D0859760

Doomsday Weapons
in the Hands of Many

DOOMSDAY WEAPONS
in the Hands of Many

The Arms Control
Challenge of the '90s

Kathleen C. Bailey

UNIVERSITY OF ILLINOIS PRESS
Urbana and Chicago

For Tina, Mama Cat, Rubah, and all the animals that so enrich our lives. We owe it to those who share our planet but who do not possess the power to reason to prevent the use of weapons of mass destruction.

© 1991 by the Board of Trustees of the University of Illinois
Manufactured in the United States of America
C 5 4 3 2 1

This book is printed on acid-free paper.

Library of Congress Cataloging-in-Publication Data

Bailey, Kathleen C.
    Doomsday weapons in the hands of many : the arms control challenge
of the '90s / Kathleen C. Bailey.
        p. cm.
    Includes index.
    ISBN 0-252-01826-5.
    1. Nuclear arms control. 2. Chemical arms control. 3. Biological
arms control. 4. Nuclear nonproliferation. I. Title.
JX1974.7.B34 1991
327.1'74—dc20   91-8081
                                                                    CIP

Contents

Acknowledgments

Special people gave their time and shared their knowledge with me during the writing of this book. Although the responsibility for the content is mine alone, I would like to thank the following people for their comments on one or more chapters: Bob Barker, Jerry Mullins, Andrea Bailey, Michael Rosenthal, Stephen P. Cohen, Joe Smaldone, Hugh Stringer, Bill Dee, Barb Seiders, Bob Mikulak, Ted Gold, Tony Parmee, George Anzelon, John Harvey, Mike Elleman, Giovanni Snidle, Tom Morgan, and Dave Nydam. Also, Keith Colliver and Randy Rydell provided valuable assistance in locating sources.

Introduction

The probability is increasing daily that the lives of people in any country on this earth could be drastically affected—even ended—by a weapon of mass destruction.[1] Many nations are now capable of making and using nuclear, chemical, biological, and toxin weapons, as well as acquiring ballistic or cruise missiles that can deliver these potent warheads to great distances without reliance on aircraft.

There are several reasons why the danger posed by proliferation is so serious.

1. *The number, location, and character-of-government of proliferant countries is highly threatening.*

The number of countries that possess weapons of mass destruction is rapidly increasing. Although dire predictions of rampant nuclear proliferation made in the late 1960s have not come true, Israel, India, and Pakistan have acquired nuclear weapons capability since that time. In addition, a host of nations have sophisticated nuclear energy programs that could be turned to weapons purposes, given a political decision to do so.

The most frightening developments have taken place in the area of chemical and biological weapons and their delivery systems. At least twenty nations are known to have or to be developing chemical weapons and more than a dozen appear to be working on biological and/or toxin weapons. Because of the difficulties associated with detecting secret chemical, biological, and toxin weapons programs, there may be many more than this. Many of the countries known to be working on such weapons are buying or developing missile delivery systems as well.

The likelihood that weapons of mass destruction will be used increases with the number of countries that have them. The danger is further enhanced by the fact that many of the weapons-possessing countries are located in regions of conflict. The Middle East is the prime example. Iraq acquired and used chemical weapons in its war with Iran, and in response, Iran developed and used them too. Subsequently, Iraq menaced Israel with its chemical weapons capability, challenging Israel's nuclear weapons capability. Soon thereafter, following its annexation of Kuwait, Iraq threatened the multinational force assembled to protect Saudi Arabia.

The danger that weapons of mass destruction will be used is also affected by the relative stability of a country's government or the mental balance of its ruler. While some have argued that possession of nuclear weapons might make a ruler or state behave more responsibly, evidence indicates otherwise. Ruthlessness or lack of sanity has led some Middle Eastern leaders to use chemical weapons on their own populations or to engage in terrorism. This lends credibility to the argument that some leaders might be irresponsible with a weapon of mass destruction, if one were at hand.

2. *Terrorist organizations may use such weapons.*

Growth in the number and sophistication of terrorist organizations has added to the danger posed by proliferation. Terrorists have demonstrated their willingness to kill somewhat indiscriminately large numbers of people, and to them weapons of mass destruction are attractive both for blackmail and actual use. Although most terrorists would probably steal such weapons, it is not beyond their means to develop these weapons themselves—especially chemical, biological, or toxin weapons.

3. *The weapons of proliferants are likely to be neither safe nor secure.*

The possibility that terrorists could steal a weapon of mass destruction depends, to a great extent, on how seriously the armed country has taken the responsibility for security. The possibility of accidental detonation depends on the technical sophistication of safety features. Inadequate attention to safety and security may make the first victims of proliferation the citizens of the country or region that developed the weapon.

The United States, for example, constructs its weapons in a way that prevents their accidental use or their use in case of theft. Complex controls are exercised in storing, moving, or deploying chemical and nuclear weapons so that unauthorized use is exceedingly difficult, probably even impossible. (The United States does not have biological or toxin weapons.) These controls and measures have been developed at significant cost over a period of many years. Will nations with scant resources have the technical capability, motivation, and financial wherewithall to develop such safety and security? Even if they try, it is unlikely that they will be able to achieve adequate, technically sophisticated measures.

4. *International norms against proliferation have been and are being eroded.*

The use of chemical weapons provides the most recent and best-known example of eroding norms. The 1925 Geneva Protocol prohibits their use, although it does not prohibit their production and stockpiling. Iraq, a signatory of the protocol, used chemical weapons against Iran (also a signatory), which responded in kind. Neither country suffered any sanctions from the international community, and this sent a signal to others that use of chemical weapons is an offense without much consequence.

In the realm of nuclear proliferation, the Treaty on the Non-Proliferation of Nuclear Weapons (NPT) is at risk. Egypt, a party to the NPT, has stated that it cannot continue to show restraint on nuclear weapons if Israel does not also become a party to the treaty. Egyptian withdrawal from the NPT would be a terrific blow to the treaty and perhaps would stimulate other nations, such as the Arab nations that have only recently adhered to it, to withdraw also. The willingness of the United States to ignore Israel's proliferation has undermined the norm the NPT strove to achieve.

The United States is not the only country whose responses to acts of proliferation have been inadequate. In 1974, India detonated a nuclear explosive. President Bhutto of Pakistan, who had declared in 1965 that the people of his country would eat grass to develop a nuclear weapons capability to match India's, set his country on the nuclear weapons path as well. Just over a decade later, Pakistan had the essentials. International reactions have been either indifferent (some nations did not even denounce the acts) or unbalanced (i.e., condemning one country but not the other). Other nations, observing that Israel, India, and Pakistan are not penalized for nuclear proliferation, query why they should continue to forgo such weapons.

The norms against nuclear proliferation are endangered by an even more insidious threat: noncompliance with the NPT by its parties. North Korea, for example, is obligated to conclude a safeguards agreement whereby its nuclear facilities would be regularly inspected to assure they are used for peaceful purposes only. As of early 1991, North Korea has not done so. This is of particular concern because North Korea has facilities that are suspected of being part of a nuclear weapons development effort. The refusal to effect safeguards while remaining party to the NPT diminishes the authority and credibility of the treaty, which may license other NPT signatories to ignore their obligations.

5. *Proliferation now includes delivery capability.*

Without a means of delivery, the value of nuclear, chemical, biological, and toxin warheads is limited. They might be delivered with aircraft, but not with high confidence because of well-developed air defense capabilities in many countries. Clandestine delivery of weapons with timers in suitcases, commercial aircraft, or ships is also difficult. With the proliferation of ballistic and cruise missiles, the confident delivery of warheads becomes relatively easy.

Ballistic and cruise missiles also increase the range to which an aggressor can reach. Middle Eastern missiles can now reach Europe and the Soviet Union; Indian missiles will soon be able to do so as well. North Korean missiles may threaten Japan. Thus, the notion of confined regional conflict due to limitations of range is outmoded.

6. *Motivations to proliferate will increase as alliances disintegrate.*

From the end of World War II to mid-1990, there was a balance of power between the two major blocs possessing weapons of mass destruction and their delivery capabilities. With the changes in Eastern Europe and the redefinition, if not the disintegration, of the two major defense alliances, many countries will rethink their security positions. They may face threats from proliferant countries of the Middle East or from European neighbors. They could conclude, as France did under Charles de Gaulle in the 1960s, that self-reliance and the development of nuclear and/or chemical weapons are the best options.

Many industrialized countries in the East and West possess the technical capability to build weapons of mass destruction as well as missile delivery systems. Several already possess highly developed nuclear and/or chemical industries and are capable of developing warheads independently.

The six reasons cited for concern about proliferation indicate that the problem is very serious. Yet, despite the increasing risks associated with proliferation, there is complacency toward the problem, not only in the United States and Western Europe but in the entire international community. Particularly surprising is the complacency of developing countries and members of the Nonaligned Movement, which would be most vulnerable to a regional war involving weapons of mass destruction.

In part, the reason for such complacency toward proliferation stems from a consuming preoccupation with superpower arms control. Institutions, the press, the public, and, most of all, government leaders, are to blame. So intense has been the desire to restrain and reduce superpower nuclear, chemical, and conventional forces that control of the same weapons in other countries has been given scant attention.

In comparison to the U.S.-Soviet Strategic Arms Reduction Talks, issues such as Pakistan's nuclear weapons program, India's ballistic missiles, and the widespread development of chemical weapons have been given sparse attention in the American media. Only when chemical weapons became an issue in the Persian Gulf crisis did the media begin to cover the proliferation issue. Even then, the coverage was primarily Iraq-specific; it did not address the numerous other countries with chemical weapons programs. The media in Europe, Asia, Latin America, and Africa also give inadequate attention to proliferation.

In the United States, Congress and the governmental bureaucracy also focus on U.S.-Soviet arms control. Career diplomats know, for example, that, as far as their futures go, it is better to be involved in arms control negotiations with the USSR than in efforts to address proliferation. The preoccupation with superpower arms control is understandable, of course. The USSR has long been the only nation that could destroy the United States, and vice versa. But now others have the means to cause massive physical destruction and/or loss of life, and it is time for the arms control process to shift with this reality.

Non-Soviet weapons of mass destruction can be used in a variety of ways against the United States and its allies. American forces abroad could be hit on land or at sea. A French-made Exocet missile fired by Iraq hit an American vessel in the Persian Gulf in 1987 during the Iran-Iraq war. Thirty-seven American sailors died; and if the missile had had a chemical or biological warhead, there might have been no survivors.

Possession of intermediate-range ballistic missiles is now widespread. India, Iraq, Israel, North Korea, and Saudi Arabia have bought or developed ballistic missiles that can travel in excess of five hundred kilometers. Argentina, Brazil, Egypt, Pakistan, South Africa, Syria, and others have missile development programs that could soon culminate in a deployable system with an even greater range. Targets within

Western Europe and the Soviet Union are already within range. Making matters worse, any one of the possessor nations might give or sell a missile, or the technology to build it, to a friend or ally. If Libya were able to steal, buy, or borrow a ballistic missile, for example, Italy—a country where American forces are based—would be within range.

The continental United States itself is not beyond threat. For example, India has developed a satellite launch vehicle (which uses essentially the same technology as that for ballistic missiles) capable of delivering warheads to within intercontinental range. While there is no reason today for India to strike the United States, this may not always be the case. Iraq has made progress on SLV technology as well, testing it on December 5, 1989. Other nations are not far behind. America need not be at war with any of these nations for the danger of an accidental launch, or a purposeful launch by an irresponsible ruler, to exist.

In the case of developing and nonaligned countries, it is not readily apparent why they express little concern for proliferation, in contrast to their activism regarding superpower arms control. It is the poorer and developing countries that are proliferating, and it is their populations and land that are probably most threatened. Perhaps it has been too difficult politically for these countries to focus on proliferation in their midst, but it is time for this to change.

Proliferation now constitutes one of the most serious threats to international peace and stability, as well as to U.S. national security. It should become the focus of multinational and bilateral arms control efforts before it is too late. This book is intended to describe the scope and nature of the proliferation problem and to offer some ideas as to what might be done to address it. Three questions must be asked: How hard is it to acquire weapons of mass destruction (nuclear, chemical, biological, or toxin) and the attendant delivery systems (ballistic or cruise missiles)? Which countries are currently trying to acquire them? Is there anything that the United States and other countries might do to better confront and solve this problem?

NOTE

1. In 1979 testimony before the Senate on the SALT II Treaty, the U.S. government provided input regarding the definition of the phrase "weapons of mass destruction." Material supplied for the Senate Record included a resolution adopted by the UN Commission for Conventional Armaments on August

2, 1948, which was adopted by both the United States and the Soviet Union. The commission resolved to advise the UN Security Council "that it considers that all armaments and armed forces, except atomic weapons and weapons of mass destruction, fall within its jurisdiction and that weapons of mass destruction should be defined to include atomic explosive weapons, radioactive material weapons, lethal chemical and biological weapons, and any weapons developed in the future which have characteristics comparable in destructive effect to those of the atomic bomb or other weapons mentioned above." This definition is cited and discussed in Alan M. Jones, "Implications of Arms Control Agreements and Negotiations for Space-based BMD Lasers," in *Laser Weapons in Space: Policy and Doctrine*, ed. Keith B. Payne (Boulder: Westview Press, 1983), p. 78. The definition of weapons of mass destruction is also made clear in the text of the Convention on the Prohibition of the Development, Production, and the Stockpiling of Bacteriological (Biological) and Toxin Weapons, and on Their Destruction: "such dangerous weapons of mass destruction as those using chemical or bacteriological (biological) agents."

1

Nuclear Weapons: Hard to Develop?

To develop a nuclear weapon, a nation must successfully acquire a sufficient quantity of weapons-usable fissile material, high explosives and related explosives technology, and a workable design for a nuclear explosive device. It is difficult for non–nuclear weapons states to import the materials and knowledge necessary for nuclear weapons development. Countries that do export nuclear technology usually include safeguards that deter nonpeaceful uses.

Despite the political and technical obstacles to designing nuclear weapons, most nations today have a cadre of well-educated scientists who could, with a dedicated effort, master the mysteries of the atom bomb. A significant amount of information on nuclear physics and chemistry, high explosives manufacture and performance, and other relevant topics is openly available for their use. Furthermore, most nations have computer capability far beyond what was available to the designers of the first American nuclear weapon. The greatest obstacle to countries developing nuclear weapons has been producing fissile material, which is very costly and technically difficult, though much easier today than it was in the 1940s.

Fissile Material

Fissile material comprises the core of a nuclear explosive. It contains atoms that, when properly configured by high explosive and then bombarded with neutrons, will split. This releases energy and more neutrons that propagate the process. A series of rapidly multiplying fissions is a nuclear chain reaction, which releases tremendous heat and energy. Theoretically, a number of elements and isotopes could be used to form the core of a nuclear explosive, but the two most practical are uranium 235 (U-235) and plutonium 239 (Pu-239).

Separation of U-235, an isotope naturally occurring in uranium ore (0.7 percent of uranium atoms are U-235), is referred to as enrichment. There are four primary methods of uranium enrichment: gaseous diffusion, centrifuge, laser isotope, and chemical exchange.

The design of a uranium enrichment facility was a tremendously complex task for the United States and the other nations that first developed the technology indigenously. A country with limited scientific and technical resources is very unlikely to be able to design and build a workable enrichment facility because of the tremendous complexity not only of the chemical and industrial processes involved but also the extraordinary materials science required. Pakistan, for example, probably would not have been able to establish its successful centrifuge enrichment plant had it not stolen the engineering and other necessary documentation from a European plant. (This is discussed in greater detail in Chapter 2.) Brazil, a developing country with an industrial infrastructure far greater than Pakistan's, also has built a centrifuge enrichment facility but without the same level of success. Iraq, probably using a centrifuge design the same or similar to Brazil's, has also been struggling to enrich uranium. Iraq reportedly has been importing equipment from West Germany that would be useful in manufacturing centrifuges.[1]

In the future, it is likely that other nations will acquire the ability to enrich uranium via centrifuge. Chemical exchange (chemex) may also appeal to future proliferators because it is technically fairly easy. Japan is currently experimenting with chemex to determine whether it is more economical than other processes. At present, probably because there are no commercial-scale chemex facilities in operation, this technology is not a popular option.

Gaseous diffusion is very difficult and expensive. The most complex problem is the design of a membrane through which uranium-235 isotopes will pass more quickly than U-238. Though Argentina has claimed success enriching U-235 to at least a level of 20 percent using gaseous diffusion, few nations have chosen this route.

Laser isotope separation is even more demanding technically. Although it is a proven technology, it is not likely that it will be used in the foreseeable future except perhaps by technically advanced nations such as Israel.

Regardless of the method it chooses, a nation must obtain or produce a design for the enrichment plant, procure specialized materials and components to build the facility, and then operate it. None of these steps is simple. Additionally, the nation must somehow obtain natural uranium, mill it, and chemically convert it. These processes are straightforward and well documented; they are particularly easy for any nation with a mining industry and experience in basic chemical industry.

In addition to enriched uranium (U-235), plutonium-239 can be used as the fissile material for a nuclear explosive. Plutonium 239 does not occur naturally in the environment, unlike U-235. It is created in nuclear reactors when a U-238 atom absorbs a neutron. Reactors fueled with natural uranium are the optimum producers of Pu-239. However, reactors with enriched uranium fuel, which is usually 97 percent U-238, can also be used to produce plutonium for weapons. Pu-239 can also be produced when a "blanket" of U-238 is placed around the outside of a reactor core.

Should a nation choose to develop its own natural uranium reactor as a source of Pu-239, it must undertake several difficult and costly tasks. This discussion is premised on the idea that a nation is attempting to develop a nuclear weapon and is trying to assure that its entire plutonium production program is indigenous—unfettered by export controls or safeguards. (It is not required that the program be totally indigenous, however. Many of the steps can be—and have been—circumvented by purchasing materials, technology, and facilities from other nations.)

First, a workable natural uranium reactor must be designed, a relatively easy task given the availability of detailed designs, particularly for graphite reactors. Although vast amounts of literature detail reactor design problems and solutions, difficult engineering is involved. There must be a thorough understanding of how to build the reactor, prepare uranium for fuel fabrication, fabricate fuel, obtain high-quality graphite (carbon) or heavy water moderator (discussed below), and operate the reactor safely. This whole process would cost on the order of several hundred million dollars, or less should a country cut corners on safety and wages. It is difficult to estimate the exact cost overall because the expenses of the American nuclear industry would differ from those of a less-developed country where standards are more lax.

Preparing uranium for production of plutonium-239 involves some of the same steps as those used for uranium enrichment. That is, natural uranium must be obtained and milled to extract uranium compounds, which are then chemically converted into other uranium compounds. These steps are well understood and documented. Although the tasks are not highly complex, they require substantial capital investment.

The next step is to fabricate fuel from the uranium, a demanding metallurgical task. Having the blueprints for an existing fuel fabrication facility and/or an experienced staff can save much time and money. There is a substantial body of literature on the processes and problems involved in manufacturing the uranium dioxide pellets or uranium metal rods that fuel the reactor.

Moderators for the reactor, whether graphite or heavy water, present manufacturing difficulties. Heavy water, or deuterium oxide, has proven particularly difficult for developing countries to produce in large quantities. India, for example, has built its own heavy water production facilities but has had so many problems that it imported heavy water illegally at least twice.[2]

Once a reactor is built, it must maximize the production of Pu-239 in a safe manner. Fuel elements—and uranium that may have been blanketed around the core—are periodically removed and allowed to cool in a tank of water in preparation for "reprocessing," or the chemical separation of the Pu-239 from the used fuel. Reprocessing is technically very challenging, primarily because of the radiological toxicity of the plutonium and other fission products in the fuel. Designing such a facility is not the most difficult task, for reprocessing technology is described openly in journals and other literature. The significant challenge is construction and operation of a full-scale facility in which the toxic materials must be handled remotely; specialized equipment and skilled operators are required.

A nation that has a functional nuclear power reactor could bypass the above-listed steps (except reprocessing) if it is willing to violate safeguards agreements and accept possible supplier cutoffs. The reactor need not be natural uranium; reactors fueled with enriched uranium also produce plutonium. However, the technical difficulties associated with separating Pu-239 from such fuel may be greater.

Which Route Is Easier?

In the past, it was generally thought that plutonium was the easier of the two fissile materials to obtain. Technical details on reprocessing were declassified by the United States and France in the 1950s, whereas information on enrichment technology was withheld. Even within the American technical community, the technology used to separate uranium isotopes in gaseous diffusion—the original method used by the United States to obtain weapons material—is kept highly secret.

Several nations have attempted to produce and separate plutonium. Argentina, Brazil, India, Israel, Pakistan, South Korea, and Taiwan[3] are countries that have tried reprocessing on a pilot scale, at a minimum. Some sought outside assistance from advanced nuclear supplier countries. Only India and Israel clearly succeeded in producing plutonium on a scale large enough to support a nuclear weapons program.

Perhaps these countries tried reprocessing because they thought it was easier, but they also had other reasons. All had either a foreign-supplied research reactor or a foreign-supplied power reactor with spent fuel containing plutonium. With only the technical hurdle of reprocessing remaining, they could circumvent the complicated process of obtaining, processing, and enriching uranium to obtain U-235 for weapons.

Reprocessing to obtain Pu-239 was a more attractive option than enriching uranium because of the popularity of nuclear energy and the notion that a complete fuel cycle is a legitimate, desirable objective for any nation. For example, prior to the late 1970s, breeder reactors—reactors that produce more plutonium than they burn—were believed by many to be the most viable, attractive alternative for energy production. It was also generally accepted that uranium would soon be depleted and that the future of nuclear energy very much depended on breeder reactors. Thus, reprocessing was seen as a legitimate and integral part of civil power reactors. Any nation that wanted reprocessing to obtain weapons materials had a cover for its real motive.

In the late 1970s, the United States rejected breeder reactors and began actively campaigning against the sale of reprocessing technology. The United States strongly opposed France's proposed sale of reprocessing technology to Pakistan; under significant international pressure from other nuclear suppliers as well, France reneged on the contract. Likewise, West Germany backed away from its plan to sell Brazil reprocessing technology. Only India and Israel, which had started their efforts much earlier and had developed significant infrastructures and capabilities of their own, succeeded in operationalizing full-scale reprocessing of plutonium.

Whether the use of plutonium or uranium is easier depends on what resources a nation already possesses and what technology it believes it can access. Pakistan, for example, first tried reprocessing because it had a functioning reactor and its spent fuel. It also assumed that France would supply reprocessing technology and equipment. When the reprocessing assistance did not materialize, Pakistan reassessed its options, obtained the blueprints for a uranium centrifuge enrichment facility, and took that route. Although it may not have abandoned the reprocessing effort as a long-term goal, it is uranium enrichment that first gave Pakistan nuclear weapons material.

Explosives Design

A plutonium bomb has a core of Pu-239 surrounded by a high explosive that, when properly detonated, squeezes the plutonium. The explosive must squeeze the plutonium until it becomes so compact, or "supercritical," that neutrons are produced and captured fast enough to sustain a chain reaction. If the chain reaction proceeds fast enough—faster than the plutonium core is blown apart by the energy produced—a nuclear explosion occurs.

There are many difficulties with plutonium weapons designs that require advanced knowledge in a variety of technical disciplines including nuclear physics, chemistry, and engineering. Correct amounts of plutonium, additional materials needed, the formation and detonation of high explosives, and the achievement of supercritical compression are only some of the technical questions that must be answered. In addition to the multitude of calculations necessary in designing a workable device, there are hurdles in manufacturing the components. Machining plutonium metal is a particularly difficult and dangerous task, for example.

One of the most crucial steps in achieving effective supercriticality is generating a simultaneous triggering of detonators which in turn set off the high explosive surrounding the fissile material. Krytrons are very fast electric switches that deliver high-voltage, high-current pulses in a fraction of a second. They are used to achieve simultaneous ignition of the high explosive to create uniform implosion.

There are a dozen or so different types of krytrons that can be used in lasers, strobe lights, and photocopy machines, but krytrons for nuclear explosives are highly sophisticated, single-use, and particularly difficult to design and manufacture. Although Iraq has claimed it can make krytrons suitable for nuclear weapons,[4] this is not likely to be true. Sophisticated krytrons are so difficult to make and so use-specific that attempts to smuggle them out of the United States by three countries— Israel, Pakistan, and Iraq—can be viewed as indicative of efforts to develop nuclear weapons capability.

A nuclear explosive using enriched uranium has many of the same problems as one using plutonium, but for U-235 a gun device is possible in which two subcritical slugs of fissionable material are slammed together by conventional explosives. When the slugs collide the total configuration becomes supercritical, a chain reaction begins, and nuclear explosion is achieved. One of the reasons a uranium design is simpler is that it may require only a few simultaneous pulses to fire the high explosive.

Designing a nuclear explosive is made faster and easier with high-performance computers, but they are not necessary. The first U.S. nuclear explosive was designed before electronic computers were available, and most current U.S. nuclear weapons were designed using computers now considered primitive.[5] Nevertheless, the United States, Western European nations, and Japan ordinarily have not provided high-performance computers to nuclear proliferant countries. Prior to 1991, a notable exception was the provision of U.S. supercomputers to India and Israel.

On December 13, 1990, the U.S. policy on provision of high-performance computers was revised. President George Bush agreed to sell Brazil, India, and China advanced computers, subject to safeguards to ensure that they be used exclusively for peaceful civilian purposes. Such controls will be exceedingly difficult to exercise, however. Short of guarding against misuse around the clock, there are few if any means of assuming peaceful use.

A country that wants the aid of high-performance computers but encounters the obstacles of export controls on safeguards has other options. It can use low-end or mid-range computers to design nuclear weapons, although calculations take longer to complete. It could also easily acquire performance accelerators that render low- and mid-range computers nearly as capable as high-performance computers.

This may even be less expensive than acquiring a high-performance computer.

Weapons Are Easier to Develop Today

Developing a nuclear weapon is easier today than it was when the United States began its effort in 1942. This is due to several factors, including the availability of information about the American program, the existence of multiple sources for relevant equipment and materials, and widespread familiarity with nuclear technology due to the prevalence of civil nuclear programs.

The availability of information on how to design and construct facilities, what pitfalls exist, and how to solve problems is remarkable. Scientists in many countries have published research of indirect and direct use to nuclear weapons development. Easily accessible computer data bases have made information available to technologists even in the most remote locations.

Education has profoundly affected the ease of engaging scientists and technologists for a weapons program. There is more pertinent knowledge being taught, and there are more students learning. Today there are courses in nuclear chemistry, physics, and engineering that were not offered two decades ago and that can prepare technical people to be directly useful upon entering a weapons program.

Equipment is a problem, however. Countries that want to purchase machinery and materials either for their fissile materials production efforts or for nuclear-related explosives encounter the obstacle of export controls. Following the signing of the Nuclear Nonproliferation Treaty in 1968, guidelines were drawn up for the international control of nuclear-related materials and equipment. Controls were further tightened after the 1974 Indian nuclear explosion, when supplier countries formed the London Suppliers Club, a cartel to curtail nuclear technology exports.

For countries without a sophisticated industrial base, much of the specialized equipment necessary to make a nuclear explosive must come from abroad. Pakistan has proved this can be done by acquiring foreign technology piecemeal, using front companies, false documentation, and a host of contorted schemes. Western companies, particularly high-technology firms in West Germany, have regularly and systematically violated export controls to provide Pakistan and others with equipment and knowledge.

Nuclear weapons are not easy to make, but they are easier to make than they were when the United States began its program over four decades ago. This is true because of the wide availability of technical knowledge, materials, and equipment. Production of fissile material, the most difficult aspect of weapons acquisition, is expensive and technically demanding, but with a dedicated effort it can be done.

NOTES

1. Charles W. Corddry, "Iraqi Progress toward Nuclear Weaponry Worries Experts on Mideast," *Baltimore Sun,* March 16, 1990, p. 16.

2. Michael R. Gordon, "Romania Is Reported in Nuclear Deal with India," *New York Times International,* April 30, 1990.

3. The case of Taiwan is cited in Leonard S. Spector, *The Undeclared Bomb* (Cambridge, Mass.: Ballinger, 1988), p. 19.

4. Paul Lewis, "Iraq Says It Made an Atom 'Trigger'," *New York Times,* May 9, 1990, p. 5.

5. U.S. nuclear weapons were designed with computers that were approximately one thousand to one hundred thousand times less powerful than modern high-performance computers, which have capability in excess of one thousand million floating-point operations per second. See Jack Worlton, "Some Myths about High-Performance Computers and Their Role in the Design of Nuclear Weapons," Technical Report No. 32, June 22, 1990, Worlton & Associates, Los Alamos, N.Mex.

2
Nuclear Proliferation: Some Examples

The 1968 Nuclear Nonproliferation Treaty (NPT) listed five nuclear weapons states—China, France, Great Britain, the United States, and the Soviet Union. Subsequent to the NPT, India openly demonstrated its nuclear weapons capability by detonating a device in 1974. There are several other nations with nuclear weapons capability, and with many others on the threshhold, the list may grow.

Other than the five nuclear weapons states, nations with advanced nuclear capabilities can be categorized generally as probable or potential nuclear weapons states or as capable-but-restrained countries. Each of these is described below.

Of greatest concern are the probable nuclear weapons states. India, Israel, and Pakistan all fit into this category. Nations that have the following combination of capabilities and motivations are considered probable nuclear weapons states:

• A successfully developed full-cycle nuclear program outside of safeguards despite severe resource problems and international political disapproval;

• Fissile material produced in a manner and amount unjustifiable for a civil nuclear program;

• Activities indicative of nuclear explosives work;

• A protracted dispute or conflict with neighbors that might provide motivation for nuclear weapons acquisition;

• Ballistic missile capabilities suitable for nuclear weapons delivery.

Potential nuclear weapons nations are those that have fairly advanced nuclear programs, but their intentions are suspect. These nations cause worry either by their refusal to undertake political commitments to refrain from nuclear proliferation or their suspicious behavior despite such assurances. This group includes Iran, Iraq, and North Korea. In the past it has included South Korea and Taiwan, and may yet again. Argentina and Brazil have also been in this category but have taken steps toward placing restraints on their nuclear programs and are committed to instituting safeguards on their nuclear facilities. South Africa is also a potential nuclear weapons state, although it has several characteristics that might make it a candidate for the list of probable nuclear weapons states.

The third category is capable-but-restrained nations. Each nation in this group could make a nuclear weapon if it made the political decision to do so. Each has a sophisticated technical infrastructure, strong economic standing, and well-developed civil nuclear capabilities. Each, however, has expressed the intention to refrain from developing nuclear weapons and takes steps to reassure others of this decision. This group includes Belgium, Italy, Japan, the Netherlands, Norway, Sweden, Switzerland, and Germany.

Any of the capable-but-restrained nations could change its commitment under different circumstances. Decisions about nuclear defense might be altered if the NPT were to unravel; if changes in NATO or the Warsaw Pact created significant conventional defense imbalances among European nations; if proliferation became widespread among less-developed countries; or if countries in key regions such as the Korean Peninsula developed nuclear weapons.

This chapter will focus on four nations: India, Pakistan, Israel, and Sweden. The first three have opted for nuclear weapons; the last one decided not to. Additionally, some factors that might lead nations to alter their decisions about nuclear weapons will be discussed.

India

In 1958, Indian leaders became aware of China's nuclear weapons development program.[1] That same year, India decided to build indigenously a plutonium reprocessing facility at Trombay. This was two years before India's first reactor, a Canadian-supplied heavy water research reactor, was to become operational. The leader of India's nuclear program at the time was Cambridge-educated Homi Bhabha, a strong advocate of Indian nuclear capability independent of safeguards. Bhabha stated that India had decided to acquire reprocessing capability in order to make a complete fuel cycle for its civil power reactors.

In 1964, two years after it had defeated India in a border war, China successfully tested a nuclear explosive. Prime Minister Shastri of India publicly stated his support for peaceful nuclear explosives.[2] Bhabha declared that India could match China's nuclear accomplishment.

In 1965, about the time that the Trombay reprocessing facility was completed, Bhabha sought permission to begin a secret effort to build a peaceful nuclear explosive. A few months later, in 1966, Bhabha was killed in a plane crash, which effectively derailed the plan. His death was a significant blow to the Indian nuclear program overall, yet the foundation had been built. The Canadian-supplied Cirus reactor and the Trombay reprocessing facility were operating. India had the fissile material for weapons.

In 1968, India made two decisions that further defined and solidified its intentions: it refused to sign the NPT, and it decided to design and build its own research reactor. The year 1971 was a crucial one. In July the U.S. government undertook rapprochement with China, using Pakistan as an intermediary. As a direct result of its insecurity, India compromised nonalignment and signed a treaty of friendship and cooperation with the Soviet Union. Meanwhile, serious domestic problems in East Pakistan (now Bangladesh) caused a flood of refugees to enter India. At the end of the year, India sent troops into Pakistan, resulting in that country's division and the formation of Bangladesh.

During this invasion, the United States sent the aircraft carrier *Enterprise* into the Bay of Bengal. Some Indians claimed that the carrier, because it was said to be "nuclear powered," was equipped with nuclear weapons and that the United States considered using them to stop the division of Pakistan. Although this was untrue, it did influence the debate over the development of nuclear weapons capability. The incident was used to counter the "doves" who argued against India's nuclear weapons program.

Despite vocal domestic opposition to a nuclear weapons program, sometime in early 1972 Prime Minister Indira Gandhi decided in secret to develop and test a nuclear explosive.[3] Throughout the rest of 1972 and 1973, Indian scientists worked to perfect a design and conducted high explosives testing. In May 1974, India successfully tested a nuclear explosive.

India used plutonium separated from the fuel from its Cirus heavy water research reactor as fissile material. The Cirus reactor, which had become fully operational in 1963, had been supplied by Canada under agreement that it be used only for peaceful purposes. India skirted this using a notion popular at the time—that there is a difference between a peaceful nuclear explosive and a nuclear weapon. India said it had detonated a peaceful nuclear explosive.

Following its nuclear test, India had to decide whether to continue testing or to stay the effort. Debate was fierce. The Indian elite always had been divided on the advisability of becoming a nuclear weapons state. The questions raised undoubtedly influenced the government's decision to refrain from follow-up nuclear testing.

Reactions in the international community had perhaps a greater impact on India's civil nuclear program. Canada was the first to respond to the Indian detonation by discontinuing all nuclear assistance. Japan also quietly suspended its foreign aid program to India. Advanced-country nuclear suppliers, a group that already had resolved to enact stricter export controls, moved quickly to form a suppliers' cartel. By 1978, the United States passed legislation that would cut off its participation in India's civil nuclear program. The cumulative effect hampered India's overall nuclear capabilities. In response, India stressed self-reliance even more and strove to produce what it formerly depended on others to supply.

Development of indigenously built reactors, heavy water production facilities, fuel fabrication, and reprocessing capabilities would give India a safeguards-free source of plutonium for explosives. India has had some difficulty in developing and building nuclear facilities, but it has succeeded. It has two heavy water power reactors operational at Kalpakkam, where it is also building another reprocessing plant. Three other small reactors are under construction. All five reactors, plus some on the drawing boards, are excellent plutonium producers.

Some of India's biggest nuclear headaches have resulted from troubles in producing heavy water. Although it has six heavy water production facilities, they cannot meet India's needs. There have been numerous problems, including major leaks. As a result, India has reportedly obtained unsafeguarded heavy water illegally. In 1983, 15 tons of heavy water from Norway, intended for use in West Germany, was diverted to Switzerland, combined with 4.7 tons from the USSR, and flown to Bombay via the United Arab Emirates. In 1986, Romania sent 12.5 tons of Norwegian heavy water to India.[4]

While there is currently no indisputable evidence that India is building a nuclear arsenal, it is clear that India is capable and prepared.

It has tested a nuclear explosive, accumulated plutonium, built a program to assure the supply of safeguard-free plutonium, and maintained a large-scale secret nuclear research establishment.

India's military behavior is expansive and proactive. India expanded its armed forces 6.2 percent from 1977 to 1987 while Pakistan's slightly declined (by .5 percent).[5] India announced in March 1990 an increase of 10.5 percent in military spending, up to $9.3 billion.[6] India's leasing of a nuclear-powered submarine from the Soviet Union can only be interpreted as power projection—an attempt to establish a broader political role through military might. And India has used this might in support of its political objectives. For example, in the 1980s Indian troops entered Sri Lanka at the request of the Sri Lankan government but remained after Sri Lanka asked them to leave. Also, India sent troops to the Maldives to prevent a coup d'etat. Given that India is keenly interested in force projection and is trying to build the size and sophistication of its armed forces, it would not be surprising if India were also engaged in nuclear weapons production.

Indian leaders consistently reject one solution to the South Asian nuclear arms race by arguing against a regional agreement to ban nuclear weapons. They claim that India is threatened by Chinese nuclear weapons and that India cannot forswear the nuclear option until there is no such threat.

India has not had a nuclear deterrent vis-à-vis China since 1964, when China first began to develop a nuclear arsenal. What could cause this to change? In 1988, an academic with close ties to the Indian government and military gave an interesting response to the question, "If India has not yet developed a nuclear arsenal in response to China's, why would it do so now?" He said that it has taken India a very long time to decide that it really wants to have a reserve of nuclear weapons and that it does not want to have "primitive" weapons capability; rather, it "wants to enter the stage" with a weapons sophistication "equal to or greater than China's." He went on to explain that India's objective is to keep its nuclear arsenal a secret until it is as large as China's and has a delivery capability to match.

Pakistan is also an increasingly important factor in India's thinking about the nuclear weapons option. In the absence of its own arsenal, India would be unable to tolerate Pakistan's possession of nuclear weapons. This is due not only to the threat but also to the prestige factor. Many developing countries view nuclear weapons as a mark of status and power. Indian academics and government officials have observed that India, or any other developing country that becomes the next acknowledged nuclear weapons state, would gain enormous political advantage. Not only would there be enhanced respect from neighbors but there would be greater international clout. India would not want Pakistan to have such prominence while it did not.

The United States is also a factor in Indian nuclear issues. Indian government officials have stated that India will eventually need a nuclear deterrent against the United States. Such officials have mentioned America's presence in Pakistan in 1971 as the basis for their reasoning. Many Indians cite as fact that the USS *Enterprise* "was ordered to move against India in pursuance of US commitment to come to the assistance of Pakistan" and "President Nixon considered using nuclear weapons at the time."[7] Air Commander Jasjit Singh of the Indian Institute for Defence Studies and Analyses, a strategic thinker whose views influence and reflect the thinking of Indian leadership, couples this argument with the notion that nuclear weapons states target India. "New and tailored nuclear weapons are being developed by the US for contingencies and conflicts in territories of the developing countries," Singh states.[8]

In a similar vein, one of the foremost opinion leaders on the subject of the Indian nuclear option, K. Subrahmanyam, has argued: "Since the probability of use of nuclear weapons, so long as they are treated as legitimate weapons of war, are higher in situations of asymmetry it creates pressures on non-nuclear weapon states, which are in a position to do so, to acquire nuclear weapons to create a sense of deterrence on interventionist nations armed with nuclear weapons. Those who subscribe to the belief system of nuclear deterrence can be deterred only by nuclear weapons."[9] He further notes, "the thesis that nuclear deterrence has sustained peace in the industrialised world will make it difficult for leading nuclear-capable developing nations not to adopt the strategy of the dominant nations of the international system."[10]

Singh and Subrahmanyam have both argued that India needs nuclear weapons, one reason being the need for a deterrent against the U.S. nuclear arsenal. Fear that U.S. technical developments such as the "brilliant pebbles" strategic defense system—an American proposal to place missile defenses in space—will nullify Indian capabilities has led both men to argue against so-called vertical proliferation. (They define vertical proliferation as the technological improvement of nuclear weapons and their delivery systems.)

Essentially, Singh and Subrahmanyam argue that nuclear weapons states must put a freeze on nuclear testing, defense capabilities such as the Strategic Defense Initiative, and other high-technology weapons research. Nonnuclear weapons states will then be able to acquire and improve their nuclear capabilities until equilibrium is reached. At that point all sides could proceed to get rid of nuclear weapons. While the positions of "hawks" such as Singh and Subrahmanyam are not supported by the Indian government, many Indian officials are sympathetic to their thinking. What could prompt these officials to openly advocate a nuclear arsenal for India?

If India were to engage in conflict where the use of nuclear weapons was threatened directly or indirectly, India would almost certainly change its nuclear policy. Other than this, India would most likely develop a nuclear arsenal if yet another country developed nuclear weapons. India would probably try to prove its own nuclear prowess. It might conduct another nuclear test or publicly declare or initiate a nuclear arsenal.

In conclusion, India's nuclear weapons program, while initially a response to Chinese nuclear weapons, is a product of multiple motives. A primary driving force has been India's military ambitions, including its desire to project its influence over the entire region, from eastern Africa to Australia. Whereas national pride and security interests were paramount in establishing the Indian nuclear program, it is now seen as a means of obtaining political stature in the global context; it is a political as well as a military tool.

Pakistan

Even before India refused to join the NPT in 1968, Pakistan was convinced that India was intent on building nuclear weapons. As early as 1965, Pakistan made clear that its response would be the acquisition of its own nuclear weapon. During an interview with a British newspaper, Foreign Minister Zulfikar Ali Bhutto was asked what Pakistan's response would be if India were to "go nuclear." He responded, "Then we should have to eat grass and get one, or buy one, of our own."[11] In 1967, Bhutto argued that Pakistan had to prepare a nuclear deterrent because India was determined to detonate a nuclear bomb.[12] Relations with India remained poor, and Pakistan's fear of India drove it to acquire nuclear weapons capability. Pakistan's defeat and division in 1971 at the hands of India further stimulated Pakistan's nuclear ambitions.

Pakistan first tried to obtain fissile material for a nuclear explosive by following the same route it knew India to be taking—acquisition of plutonium. Although its civil nuclear power program did not justify the expense and effort of obtaining a plutonium reprocessing capability, Pakistan sought to buy one. Shortly after the 1972 start-up of Pakistan's Canadian-supplied Karachi Nuclear Power Plant (KANUPP)—a heavy water power reactor—discussions were initiated with France to acquire reprocessing technology, equipment, and facilities.

India's 1974 nuclear test profoundly jolted Pakistan, which stepped up its efforts to acquire reprocessing technology and signed a contract with France six months later. Although some technology was transferred under the agreement, key parts of the contract were never fulfilled. The United States and other nations concerned about Pakistan's nuclear intentions pressured France, which ceased helping Pakistan in 1978.

Meanwhile, Pakistan also had begun to experiment with uranium enrichment to obtain fissile material. Dr. Abdul Qadeer Khan, a Pakistani who worked at the uranium enrichment facility at Almelo in the Netherlands, headed the operation. Almelo is a commercial plant that uses centrifuges to make enriched uranium for power reactors. Khan brought to Pakistan substantial knowledge, including blueprints and a list of key suppliers of components, for the construction of a centrifuge enrichment facility. As the designs were from an operational facility, there was no doubt that they would work.

Although Pakistan suffered from lack of money and a deficient technical infrastructure, it made fairly rapid progress in building its enrichment plant at Kahuta. At first the project was hampered by lack of organization and, particularly, lack of imported equipment and materials. Imposition of export controls by nuclear suppliers created serious barriers to Pakistan's efforts. Ultimately, whatever Pakistan could not make itself, it imported. Export controls were cleverly circumvented by a variety of means. False bills of lading, transshipment through multiple countries, and other nefarious tricks were employed to get what was needed. As Pakistani capabilities grew, and as an enrichment-dedicated infrastructure was developed, the program was increasingly able to import basic materials and assemble them in Pakistan. This meant that Pakistan could diversify its acquisitions activities to countries other than the traditional nuclear suppliers. Some suppliers were developing countries, and others were industrialized.

In 1984 Pakistan announced its successful production of enriched uranium, made significant progress in getting high explosives and related technology, and obtained invaluable assistance from China.[13] On June 25, 1984, Senator Alan Cranston identified the following causes for concern:

• Pakistani operation and expansion of the Kahuta uranium enrichment facility;

• Tests of an unsafeguarded pilot reprocessing facility for plutonium separation;

• Expansion of the Pakistani nuclear weapons design team at the town of Wah and a step-up of imports of nuclear warhead components;

• Chronic failures in the safeguards system at the KANUPP reactor.[14]

Pakistan consistently demonstrated that it was unwilling to stop its quest for nuclear weapons capability. The United States sought Pakistani assurance at the highest levels that it would not enrich uranium above 5 percent. Pakistani leaders agreed but later broke their word.[15]

Not only did Pakistan produce highly enriched uranium usable in weapons, it continued illegally to acquire foreign technology with which to build weapons. In 1985, for example, a Pakistani national, in violation of U.S. law, attempted to export krytrons, high-speed switches suitable for detonating nuclear explosives. From 1981 through 1988, Pakistan illegally imported technology for manufacturing nuclear fuel rods and for collecting and purifying tritium gas.[16]

It is clear that Pakistan has acquired nuclear materials and is capable of making nuclear weapons. In early 1988, a U.S. government official stated, "Pakistan has acquired the technical capabilities needed to possess a nuclear explosive device, but so far has not made the political decision to do so, and some essential steps remain to be taken, if the political decision were made."[17] How does one know when the political decision has been made? How can one tell when the essential steps are taken? What are the essential steps?

To understand what essential steps remain to be taken, one must analyze what has been done already. It is clear that Pakistan has the requisite fissile material. In 1988, a report to the Committee on Foreign Relations of the U.S. Senate stated, "At current levels of operation, Kahuta [site of the Pakistani uranium enrichment facility] may be able to produce enough weapons-grade uranium for one to three nuclear explosive devices annually."[18] So, the essential step remaining is not the production of weapons-grade fissile materials.

Neither is the essential step the complete assembly of a device. In determining whether or not Pakistan possesses a nuclear device, it does not matter whether all the components are assembled, only that they exist. As the legal advisor of the State Department said: "A state may possess a nuclear explosive device, and yet maintain it in an unassembled form for safety reasons or to maintain effective command and control over its use for other purposes. The fact that a state does not have an assembled device would not, therefore, necessarily mean that it does not possess a device under the statutory standard."[19] Thus, the question is not whether Pakistan has fissile materials but whether Pakistan has taken the steps between acquisition of fissile material and weapon assembly. The question is whether the fissile material exists in a form and shape that is workable in a nuclear explosive.

How would the United States know whether Pakistan had such components? If Pakistan conducted a nuclear test on its own soil, the United States would know. Short of that, it must look at the available evidence and decide whether it is more likely than not that Pakistan has made such components. The nature of intelligence, however, is often such that there are conflicting pieces of evidence. Policymakers who did not want to conclude that Pakistan possessed nuclear weapons were motivated to give it the benefit of the doubt. Only irrefutable evidence that Pakistani nuclear components actually exist would convince them. In September 1990, the evidence that Pakistan possesses nuclear weapons was adjudged to be convincing. President Bush declined to certify to Congress that Pakistan does not possess such weapons. This certification, by law, is necessary before any U.S. assistance can be released to Pakistan.

In conclusion, Pakistan is categorized as a probable nuclear weapon state. It spent significant resources to develop a complete nuclear program outside international safeguards, and it was willing to lie and break the law to do so. It has produced highly enriched uranium in significant quantities, with no civil nuclear power program to justify doing so. It has attempted to import nuclear weapons components in circumvention of law. Disputes with India, which Pakistan believes to have nuclear weapons, is a rationale for the effort. Finally, Pakistan is seeking ballistic missile delivery capability.

Israel

In 1949, the Israeli Defense Ministry established a department for nuclear research and development at the Weizmann Institute at Rehovoth.[20] One of the first efforts of the department was to create a process for the production of heavy water for natural uranium–fueled reactors.[21]

In June 1952, Israel secretly created its Atomic Energy Commission under the control of the Ministry of Defense. Large numbers of Israelis were sent abroad to study physics, chemistry, and engineering; many were trained in the United States and France, two countries that also became the primary suppliers of nuclear technology to Israel in the 1950s. By 1960, Israel had begun operation of its first small, safeguarded research reactor, which was provided by the United States.

Israel's relationship with France was central to its development of nuclear weapons capability. In 1953, when France was still working to develop its own nuclear weapons, Israel and France signed a nuclear cooperation agreement that led to significant technology exchange. France received computers and technology of US origin for production of heavy water[22] and built a heavy water reactor and a reprocessing facility at Dimona, Israel.

Construction on the Dimona reactor began in 1958 and was kept secret until 1960. Nominally, it is a twenty-four-megawatt reactor, but it is operated at least at a forty-megawatt level. Dimona, which is not safeguarded, began operation in 1962. The reprocessing facility, located deep underground, was not completed until around 1966.

Israel did not have sufficient domestic sources of uranium to fuel Dimona, so it had to obtain foreign ore. Also, it needed at least twenty tons of heavy water, more than it could make with its small facility at Rehovoth. Through various schemes, Israel succeeded in acquiring uranium and heavy water. It is very probable that uranium was supplied through Western European firms by South Africa. Since the uranium was acquired surreptitiously, no safeguards were attached.

Israel may have received some heavy water from France. However, more is known about a controversial transaction in which Norway supplied 22 tons of heavy water in 1959. Although Norway attached bilateral safeguards that required peaceful uses only and periodical inspection of the heavy water, it is likely that the heavy water was used in the Dimona reactor to produce plutonium for weapons purposes. When news of Dimona's activities received media attention in 1987,

Norway attempted to inspect the heavy water it had supplied. Israel refused. In April 1990, the two countries reached a tentative agreement for 10.5 metric tons to be resold to Norway for $1.8 million.[23] Even if one assumes that there have been substantial operating losses, Israel is still left with several tons of Norwegian heavy water that should have been safeguarded but will no longer be.

There is no logical explanation for Israel's tremendous plutonium production other than its use in nuclear weapons. Israel has no breeder reactor program or civil nuclear energy program of any type. Perhaps the most telling evidence of Israel's intentions, however, comes from testimony provided by Mordechai Vanunu, who worked at Dimona as a technician for eight years.

Vanunu supplied photographs of Israeli nuclear weapons models, as well as details on the activities at Dimona, to the London *Sunday Times*.[24] Suspicious reporters brought in Dr. Frank Barnaby, a nuclear physicist who had formerly worked with the British nuclear weapons establishment and was director of the Swedish International Peace Research Institute. Barnaby debriefed Vanunu over two days. He was convinced that Vanunu's account of Dimona was real. Although Vanunu was kidnapped, tried, and sentenced to prison by the Israeli government before he could provide additional details, his story provides significant insight into Israeli technological capabilities.

Vanunu told of working in Israel's plutonium reprocessing facility, an eight-story building of which six stories are underground. He gave extensive details on the facility, designated Machon 2. Vanunu's revelations confirmed information shared by Francis Perrin, head of France's nuclear weapons program from 1951 through 1970. Perrin said, "In 1957, we agreed to build a reactor and a chemical plant for the production of plutonium. We wanted to help Israel. We knew the plutonium could be used for a bomb but we considered also that it could be used for peaceful purposes."[25] Perrin also confirmed another revelation drawn from Vanunu's materials—that Israel has credible nuclear weapons designs. Vanunu provided photographs of nuclear weapons models which he had taken while at Dimona. According to Perrin, "They show full scale models of bomb components and in one case an actual component made of lithium deuteride being machined into the shape of a large hemispherical shell."[26] Nuclear physicists who examined the photos concluded that Israel had a credible thermonuclear weapon design.[27]

Israel's original nuclear explosive design probably was developed in cooperation with France. Perrin said that the two countries worked together on design and development of nuclear weapons in the 1950s. (France successfully tested a nuclear explosive in 1960.) Additional indirect assistance may have come through U.S.-Israeli interactions. Israeli scientists frequently met American nuclear weapons designers at scientific meetings and in visits to U.S. weapons laboratories.

If Israel did have access to French weapons testing data, it probably had high confidence in its designs and felt no need for testing. However, significant improvements in design, including efforts to make the weapons smaller, would almost certainly require testing. There has been speculation that Israel, in cooperation with South Africa, tested a nuclear explosive in September 1979. The U.S. Vela satellite observed in the south Atlantic Ocean near South Africa activities that would be consistent with nuclear testing.

Some nuclear weapons design improvements can be developed with fair confidence on computers. Because it has acquired high-performance computer capabilities from the United States, including a supercomputer, Israel can model many of the changes it might want to make. The more sophisticated the changes, however, the more likely testing would be necessary.

The Israeli nuclear weapons program, like those of India and Pakistan, has had to rely on some foreign imports. For example, Israel was not able to manufacture all the components needed to build nuclear explosives. Like Pakistan, it sought to obtain krytrons—high-speed electronic switches—illegally from the United States. A man caught smuggling 800 krytrons to Israel in 1985 fled before he could be tried or give further information.

In conclusion, Israel fits the profile of a probable nuclear weapons state. It spent scarce resources to develop a complete nuclear fuel cycle; it produces plutonium but has no civil nuclear program; it may have tested nuclear explosives; it is obviously in conflict and has its very existence threatened; and it has developed ballistic missile delivery systems. Israel has not overtly tested a nuclear explosive, but with the evidence provided by Vanunu and Perrin, there is little doubt that it could.

Sweden

A number of countries are technically capable of building nuclear weapons but have refrained for political and/or moral reasons. Canada, Belgium, Germany, Italy, Japan, the Netherlands, Norway, Sweden, and Switzerland are some of the countries that have chosen not to develop nuclear weapons. Of these, Sweden offers one of the most interesting examples of the technically capable nonnuclear-weapons states because it once had a nuclear weapons program and abandoned it.

Sweden's nuclear weapons research was carried out at its national defense research institute, the Forsvarets Forskningsanstalt (FOA), beginning in late 1945. The work was first undertaken at the order of the supreme commander of the armed forces.[28] Initial research used funds reallocated to the nuclear project from other defense research budgets. Shortly thereafter, the Swedish Parliament was informed of the work and granted money for the research.

In 1947, AB Atomenergi was formed to develop a Swedish nuclear power industry. In 1949, a collaborative agreement between the FOA and Atomenergi was formed to intertwine research for civil and military purposes. A decision was made to design and build indigenously a heavy water research reactor. It would use Sweden's natural uranium resources and would give Swedish scientists experience in producing plutonium, although not in quantities sufficient for nuclear explosives. The one-megawatt reactor, designated R-1, became operational in July 1954.

In 1955, the question of atomic weapons led to lively debate in Parliament. Both sides had strong support. The defense minister, Torsten Nilsson, did not think it would be politically or economically beneficial to develop nuclear weapons, but many in the military supported the idea. The upshot of the debate was to postpone the decision but to continue research.

Parliamentary debate during 1956 was much the same. As discussion dragged on, research continued. High explosives tests were conducted and extensive studies of plutonium were made. It was expected that gram quantities of plutonium would be available for research use by 1957.

Although military planning documents in 1954 clearly requested authority to develop nuclear weapons, Atomenergi, which was responsible for the necessary nuclear technology, did not make military preferences paramount. In 1956, for example, although the military expressed opposition, Atomenergi accepted a U.S. offer to build an enriched uranium research reactor at a very low cost to Sweden. This thirty-megawatt reactor, which became operational in May 1960, did not fit into plans for nuclear weapons development for two reasons. First, it would be safeguarded, which would prevent the use of its nuclear materials for nonpeaceful purposes. Second, because it used enriched uranium fuel, it would not be an ideal plutonium producer.

Although the military was not happy with the decision to accept an enriched uranium, safeguarded reactor, it was assuaged by Parliament's 1956 decision to build an unsafeguarded heavy water research reactor (R-3) at Agesta.[29] This would provide enough plutonium for a few nuclear explosives. A December 1957 technical report on the R-3 reactor made it clear that the facility would not be provided with equipment necessary for frequent changes of uranium fuel. This meant that R-3 would be incapable of maximizing Pu-239 production.

In January 1958, Atomenergi submitted a report, requested by the FOA, on reactors for production of weapons-grade plutonium. Later in the year, a 200-megawatt heavy water reactor named Marviken was planned. It would produce enough plutonium to build a small stockpile of nuclear weapons.

To reprocess plutonium, a small-scale facility was built at Ursvik in 1958–59. It had some fifty glove boxes—sealed glass boxes with built-in gloves with which workers could handle dangerous materials with minimal risk of exposure. It could separate only small quantities of plutonium. In 1960, plans were drawn up for a full-scale facility to be completed as the Marviken reactor came on-line. By this time, a plan to produce plutonium for weapons was well underway.

Despite the progress and plans for plutonium production, whether Sweden would produce nuclear weapons was a topic of serious debate in the government, particularly in the Parliament during the late 1950s. Questions were raised about whether Sweden would be a target for nuclear attack if it were to have nuclear weapons. Additionally, there was growing concern about the economics of developing and maintaining the weapons.

The government gave the FOA mixed signals about whether the nuclear weapons program would continue. Although the Swedish Parliament decided against constructing nuclear weapons in 1958, money was provided for the program to continue. The 1960 budget bill postponed the decision about the program's continuation. Because plutonium was not yet available, it was decided that the matter could wait until the mid-1960s[30] after the Marviken plant would have begun operation.

Along with the delayed decision in 1960 came a government-imposed set of restrictions on weapons research. These rules limited research to that directly relevant to protection against nuclear attack. After two years, however, the rules were lifted, implying freedom to pursue broader research to those who supported a Swedish nuclear deterrent.[31]

From the lifting of the rules in 1962 to the decision to sign the Nuclear Nonproliferation Treaty in 1968, Sweden conducted significant research to develop high explosives for nuclear weapons. The FOA conducted implosion experiments, worked with a small amount of plutonium, and designed a nuclear explosive.

Despite the continued program, the probability that Sweden would actually build nuclear weapons significantly decreased in 1961. That year, the leadership of Atomengeri changed. Sigvard Eklund, who had led the company for ten years, left to become director general of the International Atomic Energy Agency. His duties there were to oversee worldwide development of peaceful uses of nuclear power and to deter nuclear weapons programs. With his move, Swedish policy shifted more toward nuclear disarmament.

In 1963, Sweden signed the Limited Test Ban Treaty, which required that all nuclear explosives tests be conducted underground. This was significant, in part because Sweden would have had a more difficult task technologically were it to test weapons under this restriction. More important, perhaps, is that underground testing would have been much more expensive.

Political obstacles to Sweden's nuclear weapons program were compounded by technical problems. The Marviken reactor had unexpected design problems, requiring the Swedes to switch to slightly enriched fuel. In turn, this required that fuel be imported, which meant that safeguards would be attached. New plans to build an independent plutonium production capability would have been too expensive, politically and financially.

Sweden's ultimate decision to abandon its nuclear weapons program resulted from a variety of factors. Politically, the notion of a Swedish nuclear arsenal was rejected by many, particularly those who envisioned a neutral Sweden actively pursuing disarmament and an end to nuclear testing. Economically, weapons were rejected by some as not being a cost-effective defense. Others said that Sweden's nuclear forces would be useless against the more heavily nuclear-armed states and would actually have the effect of inviting nuclear attack. Finally, and perhaps most important, there were serious technical problems that essentially forestalled Sweden's capability to acquire plutonium. In absence of a clearly successful plutonium production program, objections to the effort were more likely to forestall budget allocations and construction of facilities.

After Sweden signed the NPT, it abandoned nuclear weapons research except for a limited program of "protection research." There is little doubt that Sweden has the technical infrastructure and capability to produce a nuclear explosive if it chooses to do so. Even the obstacle of acquiring fissile material could be overcome rapidly if Sweden were to undertake a dedicated program, and, particularly, if it were willing to break safeguards.

Other Capable-but-Restrained States

Evidence suggests it is unlikely that Sweden would make a political decision to develop nuclear weapons. Some other countries, however, very likely may.

The reorganization of NATO and the virtual death of the Warsaw Pact have loosened security arrangements. This will have at least two effects. First, the value of the defense umbrellas provided by the alliances will be diminished. In turn, this will make it incumbent on national leaderships to contemplate how best to bolster any diminished sense of security. Second, the political-military elites in alliance countries will be liberated from constraints imposed by group decision-making processes.[32]

With the alteration in NATO and its nuclear umbrella, the threat of conventional forces again becomes a paramount concern. If force reductions are unequal or take place without effective verification, there may be additional impetus for some European countries to consider nuclear weapons, a long-acknowledged deterrent against overwhelming conventional forces.

Another stimulus to advanced-country nuclear proliferation would be the acquisition of such weapons by countries in the Third World. If the Middle East bristles with nuclear weapons, Europe will be threatened. Countries may respond with a nuclear deterrent.

Finally, there is the prestige factor. Will an economically and politically powerful Germany be satisfied with being militarily inferior to the United Kingdom and France, both of which have nuclear forces?

Europe is not the only possible locus of nuclear proliferation among technically advanced countries. Similar arguments could be made about Japan. If North Korea were to proliferate, South Korea probably would too. This scenario is not farfetched. North Korea reportedly has built a facility to reprocess spent nuclear fuel at its Yongbyon facility[33] and has reportedly received help with its nuclear program from Eastern European countries.[34] South Korea, clearly worried about North Korea's activities, is fully capable of building a reprocessing facility and pursuing nuclear weapons itself. A nuclearized Korean Peninsula would be an intolerable threat to Japan.

Conclusion

The activities of Israel, India, and Pakistan demonstrate that nuclear proliferation is a very real problem. They have developed nuclear weapons despite international pressures, the norms established by the NPT, and the efforts by nuclear supplier states to stem the flow of key technologies, materials, and equipment. Even economic pressures and bilateral leverage, applied by the United States particularly, failed. The essential lesson here is that unless something can be done to affect nations' motivations to proliferate, the process may well continue. The potential nuclear weapons states, whose well-developed nuclear programs arouse suspicion and fear, may move toward weapons capability.

Sweden is an example of a nation that left the nuclear weapons path because of its own motivations, not because of export controls, sanctions, or other forceful measures. A prolonged analysis of the political, economic, and military costs versus benefits led Sweden to its own conclusion against building a nuclear weapons arsenal.

There is great risk that changing world circumstances will make it more likely that capable-but-restrained nations will turn to nuclear weapons in the future. Possible changes include: denegration of the security provided by NATO and the Warsaw Pact; perceived reductions in the influence of the Soviet Union and the United States; further proliferation by third-world states; unraveling of the NPT; and growth in independent conventional forces. In conclusion, great care must be taken to create an environment that minimizes the insecurity of nations and dampens their motivations for nuclear weapons acquisition.

NOTES

1. Mitchell Reiss, *The Politics of Nuclear Nonproliferation* (New York: Columbia University Press, 1988), p. 220.

2. Ibid., p. 216.

3. Ibid., p. 228.

4. Michael R. Gordon, "Romania Is Reported in Nuclear Deal with India," *New York Times International,* April 30, 1990.

5. U.S. Arms Control and Disarmament Agency, *World Military Expenditures and Arms Transfers 1988,* p. 4. Available from U.S. Government Printing Office.

6. "India Announces Military Boost," *Washington Times,* March 20, 1990, p. 2.

7. Jasjit Singh, "Threat of Nuclear Weapons," in *India and the Nuclear Challenge,* ed. K. Subrahmanyam (New Delhi: Lancer International, 1986), pp. 79–80.

8. Ibid., p. 79.

9. K. Subrahmanyam, "Nuclear Deterrence," in *India and the Nuclear Challenge,* p. 106.

10. Ibid., p. 115.

11. Patrick Keatley, "The Brown Bomb," *Manchester Guardian,* March 11, 1965, p. 10.

12. Rikhi Jaipal, "The Indo-Pakistan Nuclear Options," in *India and the Nuclear Challenge,* p. 184.

13. There have been reports that China helped Pakistan with nuclear weapons design (*Nucleonics Week,* August 19, 1982) and uranium enrichment (*New York Times,* September 12, 1982).

14. *Congressional Record,* June 25, 1984 (S8144 and 8146), as cited in *Congressional Record,* vol. 135, no. 161, November 16, 1989, U.S. Senate (S15880).

15. The fact that Pakistan made this pledge and broke it is cited in *Congressional Record,* vol. 135, no. 162, November 17, 1989 (S16103).

16. "W. Germany Rocked by Nuclear Scandal," *Washington Times,* January 26, 1990, p. 8.

17. Robert A. Peck, "Testimony before the U.S. House of Representatives, Subcommittee on Asian and Pacific Affairs," February 18, 1988, pp. 11–12.

18. U.S. Senate, Committee on Foreign Relations, Staff Report, "Nuclear Proliferation in South Asia: Containing the Threat," p. 5. Available from the U.S. Government Printing Office.

19. Cited in *Congressional Record,* vol. 135, no. 161, November 16, 1989, U.S. Senate (S15880).

20. Peter Pry, *Israel's Nuclear Arsenal* (Boulder: Westview Press, 1984), p. 5.

21. Taysir N. Nashif, *Nuclear Warfare in the Middle East: Dimensions and Responsibilities* (Princeton, N.J.: Kingston Press, 1984), p. 15.

22. Pry, *Israel's Nuclear Arsenal,* p. 10.

23. John J. Fialka, "Israel Plans Sale of Heavy Water Back to Norway," *Wall Street Journal,* April 30, 1990, p. B6.

24. "Inside Dimona, Israel's Nuclear Bomb Factory," London *Sunday Times,* October 5, 1986, p 1.

25. "Israel's A Bomb," London *Sunday Times,* October 12, 1986, pp. 1, 3.

26. "Inside Dimona," p. 4.

27. Ibid.

28. Olof Forssberg, "Swedish Nuclear Weapons Research 1945–1972," Report to the Minister of Defence (unofficial translation), April 21, 1987, p. 7. Obtained by the author through the Swedish Foreign Ministry.

29. Christer Larsson, "Build a Bomb," *Ny Teknik,* no. 17, April 25, 1985, as translated in Joint Publications Research Service document WER-85-012-L, June 27, 1985, p. 18. Available through U.S. Government Printing Office.

30. Forssberg, "Swedish Nuclear Weapons," p. 9.

31. Ibid.

32. Kathleen C. Bailey, "Proliferation Could Surface as Old Alliances Sink," *Christian Science Monitor,* February 12, 1990, p. 13.

33. Peter B. de Selding, "Photos Indicate N. Korean Growth in Nuclear Ability," *Space News,* March 12–18, 1990, p. 1.

34. James Adams, "Russians Sound Nuclear Warning on North Korea," London *Sunday Times,* June 17, 1990, p. 22.

3

Nuclear Nonproliferation Policies

Nuclear nonproliferation policies can focus on either demand—attempts to build political-military barriers to a decision to develop nuclear weapons—or supply—efforts to restrict technical capabilities to build such weapons. For Germany, Japan, most of the industrialized world, South Korea, and other countries, the principal tools used to restrict demand for nuclear proliferation have been security arrangements and guarantees that obviate the necessity for nuclear weapons. NATO, in the case of West Germany, made nuclear weapons defense available but with multinational control. Likewise, the U.S. nuclear umbrella over South Korea has been central to that country's restraint on the nuclear option. Without the umbrella, South Korea would have developed nuclear weapons capability years ago.

The 1968 Nuclear Nonproliferation Treaty and the 1967 Treaty of Tlatelolco, a Latin American nonproliferation agreement, primarily work to codify rather than create restraint. They represent a political pledge not to acquire nuclear weapons.

The NPT obliges all parties that do not have nuclear weapons to forswear them. Five countries are acknowledged to be nuclear weapons states: the United States, the United Kingdom, the Soviet Union, France, and China. The first three are signatories of the NPT and are obliged to work toward disarmament and the cessation of the nuclear arms race. Nothing in the NPT inhibits the peaceful uses of nuclear energy. In fact, the NPT states that non-nuclear-weapons states that are party to the treaty shall have the benefits of nuclear energy made available to them.

The Treaty of Tlatelolco similarly commits signatories to nuclear nonproliferation. They cannot test, use, manufacture, produce, possess,

or control any nuclear weapon. Although the Tlatelolco treaty is specifically designed by and for the Latin American region, it has two proto-
cols that invite participation by extraregional states. The first protocol is
for states that control territories in Latin America. The second is for
other states to express their respect for the terms of the treaty, a central
element of which is that signatories agree not to use or threaten to use
nuclear weapons against other signatories.

A key difference between the NPT and the Tlatelolco treaty is that
the latter allows parties to conduct "peaceful nuclear explosions"—that
is, "explosions which involve devices similar to those used in nuclear
weapons" (Article 18). Because there is no technical difference between
a peaceful nuclear explosive and a nuclear weapon, the treaty has a
loophole that permits its signatories to maintain nuclear weapons programs under the guise of a peaceful effort. Although no Latin American nation has taken advantage of this loophole, it should be recalled
that India claimed its 1974 nuclear test was peaceful. Thus, it is not
unthinkable that this provision could be used by a Tlatelolco treaty
party in the future.

The credibility of commitments to forswear nuclear weapons have
been enhanced in many nations by safeguards on nuclear materials and
facilities. Under such agreements, a nation pledges that its safeguarded
nuclear assets will be used for peaceful purposes only and allows
monitoring and inspection to assure others that the promise is fulfilled.

Export controls are the primary supply-side tool used to inhibit the
technical capabilities of nations to develop nuclear weapons. Lists of
controlled materials, equipment, and technology have been drawn up
as guides to supplier nations. Overall, export controls on nuclear-
related materials and equipment from supplier nations have been fairly
effective in slowing, but not preventing, the spread of nuclear technology.
In great part this is because many of the items are not very common and
would not have other practical industrial, civil uses. Therefore attempts
to import such items are more visible and easily monitored than
attempts to import, for example, equipment and materials used for
chemical or biological weapons.

Nations that are committed to nuclear proliferation can do so despite
political barriers or constraints on the flow of technology. The problem
with political commitments is simple: some nations will refuse to undertake them. Thus, India, Pakistan, Israel, and others, which refuse to
adhere to treaties such as the NPT or the Treaty of Tlatelolco, avoid

safeguarding materials and facilities that can be used for nuclear weapons production.

Export controls, or any effort to prevent the technological advancement of nuclear weapons capability, cannot stop a dedicated effort to develop nuclear weapons. A variety of means can be used to circumvent the controls. Also, such measures cannot stymie indigenous expertise in nuclear technology in other countries.

What more can be done? This chapter summarizes some of the key motivations behind nuclear proliferation and examines some new policy efforts that might be undertaken to control it. The initiatives described have broad applicability but will be discussed using the example of Pakistan.

Summary of Motives

The principal motivations for nuclear proliferation vary from country to country, but they generally fall into a few basic categories. Security is the principal reason a country initiates a nuclear weapons program. Key decision makers become convinced that the threats a nation faces will be reduced or deterred by the possession of nuclear weapons, even though their thinking may be incomplete and erroneous. Security concerns may or may not continue to predominate once the weapons program is underway.

Prestige is also a motivation for nations to proliferate. Nuclear weapons are perceived as a symbol of technological prowess and are thus a means of gaining political clout. Another motive is the will to dominate. Nuclear weapons give an edge of military superiority over nonproliferant neighbors or adversaries. This advantage is likely to be temporary, however. History has shown that when one nation acquires nuclear weapons, its adversary tries to get them as well. The Soviet Union obtained nuclear weapons after the United States did. China, fearing the Soviet Union, followed suit, and India responded to China in the same way. Pakistan likewise has responded to India.

Bureaucratic inertia also plays a role in promoting nuclear proliferation. Once a nuclear weapons program is initiated, even when the intent is only to develop the option, it takes on a life of its own. Scientists, military officials, and political leaders support the effort with money and manpower. Institutions are built and jobs created, as in any bureaucratic organization. Ultimately, the people directly involved in the project want something to come of their efforts and thus work to bring the program from the drawing board to reality.

Sweden, like India, Pakistan, and Israel, was subject to the considerations of security, prestige, bureaucratic inertia, and perhaps the will to dominate. Yet, it abandoned its nuclear weapons program. Why? There are a variety of possible reasons, including:

• Political and military leaders were swayed by the argument that possession of nuclear weapons could add to Sweden's danger rather than to its security;

• The extraordinary expense of building a plutonium production reactor, as well as other costly aspects of the program, caused hesitation among parliamentarians;

• Many came to believe that Sweden's prestige and international political power would be enhanced more by its moral stance against nuclear weapons than by possession of them.

Crucial to Sweden's decision was that information was made available to the Swedish elite and a genuine debate, although it dragged on for two decades, was allowed to take place. Had the decision been in the hands of only a few, or conducted in secret, the outcome may have been quite different.

Perhaps analyzing the example of Sweden can help identify additional steps that might be taken to bolster nuclear nonproliferation policy. Pakistan's proliferation, one of the most difficult problems now facing the world, would also be a good example on which to focus. Before doing so, however, some nonproliferation policies that have not proven successful should be outlined.

Pakistan and Policies That Haven't Worked

Although the United States clearly failed in its efforts to prevent Pakistan from acquiring nuclear weapons capability, no nation did more to attempt to stop Pakistan. The United States tried to use both assistance and friendship as leverage. There was intense diplomatic activity, top-level attention, and sustained congressional interest in the issue. No other proliferant country has been the subject of as much U.S. domestic legislation as has Pakistan.

The United States first cut off economic and military assistance to Pakistan in 1977 to demonstrate its concern about the Pakistani nuclear program. Pakistan had struck an agreement with France to acquire a reprocessing facility, which was completely unjustified by Pakistan's nuclear energy program. The United States also pressured France to end the technology transfer.

Pakistan changed neither its behavior nor its intentions as a result of the cutoff. France, however, did respond to U.S. appeals. It suspended deliveries for the reprocessing plant after U.S. officials shared intelligence data concerning Pakistani activities and apparent intentions.[1] In response to the French move, U.S. assistance to Pakistan was restored in 1978.

Pakistan continued its efforts to obtain reprocessing capability but realized it would not succeed quickly or easily. It therefore began to work toward getting enriched uranium as well. Throughout 1978 evidence mounted that Pakistan was importing technology related to uranium enrichment, much of it from Europe. According to the 1976 Symington Amendment, the United States could not (and as of early 1991 still cannot) provide aid to a country importing uranium enrichment technology. With overwhelming evidence that Pakistan had done so, in May 1979 the United States again cut off aid to Pakistan. Again, Pakistan demonstrated no remorse and did not alter its nuclear plans. Clearly, it was willing to forsake U.S. assistance in order to arm itself with nuclear weapons. Some U.S. officials were deeply concerned that Pakistan would make up for the loss of U.S. funds by appealing to petrodollar-rich Arab states and, in return, make the "Islamic bomb" available to them. Cutting off aid to Pakistan would free it of U.S. pressures and constraints.

The Soviet invasion of Afghanistan changed the picture entirely. Pakistan was central to the U.S. government's efforts to support and supply the Afghan resistance. In order to maintain a working relationship with the Pakistani government yet continue to exert pressure regarding Pakistani nuclear developments, the United States changed its strategy. Instead of trying to punish Pakistan, U.S. policymakers turned to persuasion and inducement. The cutoff was reversed six months after it began and soon thereafter, in 1981, Congress created for Pakistan a six-year exemption from the Symington Amendment. Then the United States stepped up its diplomatic efforts to stymie Pakistan's nuclear weapons development. This may have slowed the bomb program, but it did not stop it.

The Reagan administration was deeply worried about the Pakistani nuclear program but believed that cutting off assistance would not deter it. It focused its diplomatic efforts on trying to freeze the uranium enrichment activities at a low level. President Reagan wrote President Zia Ul-Haq to say that Pakistan must not enrich uranium beyond 5 percent U-235 content, which is below weapons-usable levels. Pakistan agreed but broke its promise.[2]

Congress remained frustrated over the Pakistani situation. In 1985, it enacted yet another law, this one requiring the president to certify annually, before any aid was given, that Pakistan did not possess a nuclear explosive device and that continuing aid would significantly reduce the risk of Pakistan's proliferation. In the absence of clear-cut evidence that the components of a nuclear explosive were in Pakistan's hands, presidential certification was made annually through 1989, although not without increasing concern and doubt.

On November 18, 1988, when Reagan informed Congress of his conclusion that Pakistan did not possess a nuclear device, he stated, "I have also taken into account the fact that the statutory standard as legislated by Congress is whether Pakistan possesses a nuclear explosive device, not whether Pakistan is attempting to develop or has developed various relevant capacities." He further noted that "as Pakistan's nuclear capabilities grow, and if evidence about its activities continues to accumulate, this process of annual certification will require the President to reach judgments about the status of Pakistani nuclear activities that may be difficult or impossible to make with any degree of certainty." On October 5, 1989, President George Bush made the same judgment, adding that "Pakistan has continued its efforts to develop its unsafeguarded nuclear program."[3] There was no doubt that Pakistan had all of the technical capabilities to build a nuclear device; there was some doubt that it had done so.

The United States was intent on keeping its contacts with Pakistan, including the assistance program, in absence of conclusive intelligence about a Pakistani nuclear device. At one time, the Soviet invasion of Afghanistan was a driving force, but with the Soviet withdrawal, that concern was replaced by another: democracy. Bush declared: "I am convinced that our security relationship and assistance program are the most effective means available for us to dissuade Pakistan from acquiring nuclear explosive devices. Our assistance program is designed to help Pakistan address its substantial and legitimate security needs, thereby both reducing incentives and creating disincentives for Pakistani acquisition of nuclear explosives. It also helps to sustain Pakistan's commitment to democratic government."4 Thus, the two primary reasons given for continuing assistance were to keep Pakistan from going nuclear, if it had not already, and to keep Pakistan's fragile democracy alive.

Some in Congress argued that there was sufficient evidence of Pakistan's nuclear status to cut off aid. Such a move would make many Americans "feel good" about taking a moral stand and also would show the world that America would not aid nuclear proliferators. Any nation contemplating proliferation would have to decide whether U.S. aid was more important than nuclear weapons capability. Other reasons why the notion of cutting off aid to Pakistan gained appeal included the removal of Prime Minister Benazir Bhutto, who had been elected in December 1988 and was now charged with corruption. Although the move was purportedly done within the rules of the Pakistani constitution, Bhutto's accusers had trouble convincing the public and Bhutto's backers in the U.S. Congress that the charges were substantial. Elections were held in 1990, and Bhutto lost. Although the process was apparently forthright, a pall fell over U.S.-Pakistani relations. The stage was set for Bush to deny aid to Pakistan based on its nuclear weapons activities.

There are several reasons, however, why it was difficult for the United States to cut off aid to Pakistan. The United States feared losing a friend in a strategically important and very troubled region. Pakistan, which is in South Asia and on the edge of the Middle East, is useful in addressing problems in both regions. Also, it is one of the few countries in the area that allows U.S. ships to visit and to carry out important military-related activities. Pakistan supported U.S. policies on a number of important occasions. For example, during the Operation Desert Shield, a buildup of U.S. and other military forces in Saudi Arabia in 1990, Pakistan sent more than 5,000 troops. The support of a Moslem nation was politically important to the United States, though it caused quite a row in Pakistan.5

A cutoff of assistance to Pakistan could be detrimental to nuclear nonproliferation, even if Pakistan has already proliferated. The United States might be unable to influence Pakistan not to conduct a nuclear test, share nuclear materials or technology with other countries, develop an arsenal, or move toward additional nuclear capability. Pakistan may hesitate to move forward on any of these activities if its relationship with the United States remains strong and the United States continues to apply diplomatic pressure.

What can the United States do to improve the situation and maintain its relationship with Pakistan? Clearly, Pakistan values its nuclear program more than economic assistance; economic leverage is therefore ineffective. It also genuinely believes that a nuclear weapons program will be an asset to its security. The United States should assume that punative measures will very likely be ineffective because other nations probably will not join the United States. Both France and China have expressed their intent to help Pakistan despite U.S. pleas to join in a boycott until Pakistan drops its nuclear weapons activities. In December 1989, China agreed to build Pakistan a 300-megawatt reactor. French president François Mitterrand agreed to do the same during his visit to Pakistan in February 1990.[6]

Policy Options to Consider

Having examined the motives behind nuclear proliferation, some of the factors that led Sweden to abandon its nuclear weapons program, and some policies that have not worked, the challenge is to identify some new policy options. What might be done to help Pakistan abandon its nuclear weapons program?

Option 1: Appeal to Pakistani and Indian Military Elites

One possibility is to use Sweden's lesson: decision makers can be convinced that nuclear weapons increase rather than counter a military threat. Although unlikely, perhaps Pakistani and Indian leaders could be convinced of the same.

Currently many Pakistani and Indian journalists, strategic thinkers, and opinion leaders consider a nuclear weapons arsenal attractive. They argue that if nuclear deterrence is good for the United States and the Soviet Union, then it must be good for South Asia. Pakistan knows its potential enemy, India, already has nuclear weapons capability. India sees China and, to a lesser extent, Pakistan in the same light. In making pro-nuclear-weapons arguments, neither Pakistanis nor Indians note that the superpowers are reducing their nuclear arsenals and that Europe is being denuclearized. Also ignored is the tremendous security danger that nuclear weapons would bring to South Asia.

It is worth trying to expose Pakistani and Indian opinion leaders, the military, and policymakers responsible for defense to the counterarguments. We should not assume that a newly proliferant country has fully contemplated the consequences of nuclear weapons ownership. The United States, in particular, has had forty-five years to analyze the perils of nuclear war and the risks of introducing a nuclear threat in conflict. The United States can share this knowledge but may not be convincing if it argues the case alone; it would be in the position of arguing that what is good for the United States is not good for Pakistan or India. However, Sweden, which debated the issue for two decades, is uniquely capable of arguing against nuclear proliferation. Sweden should actively share its experiences and thinking with Pakistan and India.

Sweden, the United States, and other selected nations should send top military officials to meet with their counterparts in Pakistan and India to discuss a host of nuclear-related questions, including: the effects of nuclear combat; the limitations of nuclear deterrence; the effects of a regional nuclear arms race; the problem of keeping nuclear weapons safe and secure; the impact of nuclear weapons possession on Pakistani security; and the cost of maintaining and stationing nuclear weapons. Only military emissaries—not diplomats—could properly communicate with the target audience in Pakistan and India.

Option 2: Extend the U.S. Nuclear Umbrella

At a time when American strategic nuclear forces are being cut and nuclear weapons are unpopular, it may not seem reasonable to suggest offering nuclear protection, or so-called positive security assurances, to Pakistan. Indeed, it is not to be done lightly, but it also is not without precedent. The U.S. nuclear umbrella, for example, shields the Republic of Korea. Many are convinced that an American military presence and the nuclear shield are key reasons why South Korea has not proceeded with its own nuclear weapons capability, although it certainly has considered it.

Another way to look at the offer of nuclear protection is as an extension of current U.S. policy. The sale of sophisticated equipment such as F-16s has been justified by the notion that it adds to Pakistan's security and thus reduces the country's need for nuclear weapons. Extending the nuclear umbrella would take this policy a giant step further.

Essentially, an extensive security pact between the United States and Pakistan would mean that if Pakistan were threatened or attacked by a country possessing nuclear weapons, the United States would respond in kind on Pakistan's behalf. This would entail answering a host of complex, difficult questions, not the least of which is how to determine whether India or some other party, such as a terrorist or other enemy state, had attacked Pakistan. The United States would have to dedicate satellite assets to verify the origin of any attack against Pakistan. It would also be necessary to work with the Soviet Union to delineate the terms of the U.S.-Pakistani pact and to allay Soviet concerns.

It might even be possible to engage the Soviet Union in offering security guarantees to South Asia in exchange for nonproliferation assurances. It is in the Soviets' interests to play a positive role, as their borders are vulnerable not only to attack but to the effects of a South Asian nuclear war.

Another problem with offering nuclear security guarantees would be determining when the nuclear umbrella would be utilized. Would it be only when Pakistan fell victim to a nuclear attack, or would the concept of flexible response—possible nuclear retaliation for a conventional attack—be employed? The United States would probably have to offer conventional security guarantees as well, because Pakistan undoubtedly views its developing nuclear deterrent as a tool of last resort, to be used in a conventional war that threatened the country's existence.

What would Pakistan do in return for security guarantees? At a minimum, it first would have to place both its enriched uranium and enrichment facility under safeguards. (Indeed, they should be removed altogether, but this might be more than national pride would allow.) Second, Pakistan would have to forswear development of nuclear weapons. On-site inspections of suspect facilities would be required. Additionally, Pakistan would have to agree not to transfer its nuclear materials or know-how to other countries.

Pakistan may not agree to such terms, but the advantages would be many—primarily economic and military. In addition to freeing scarce resources from a very expensive program, the country would gain security, for it can never match India in the number of weapons or in delivery capability. In effect, Pakistan's nuclear weapons program probably would not work as a deterrent and might increase the danger faced by Pakistanis by stimulating India to increase its nuclear arsenal (if one already exists.) It may also have the effect of prompting India to use nuclear weapons in the event of war.

Option 3: Seek Regional Agreement on Delivery Systems

India and Pakistan both have aircraft capable of delivering nuclear weapons and also good air defense capabilities. Still, aircraft are not only interceptable but are subject to pilot error. A far more threatening delivery vehicle is an intermediate range ballistic missile (IRBM) or a cruise missile. India already has developed and successfully tested an IRBM, and Pakistan is trying to do the same. India has expressed interest in cruise missiles as well.

The South Asian nuclear arms race would be set back if IRBMs and cruise missiles were removed from the scene. The United States could, with the help of the Soviet Union, seek to engage Pakistan and India in a bilateral, or regional, ban on such missiles. To avoid some of the acrimony when "haves" try to get "have nots" to give up a military capability, the regional missile ban could be modeled on the U.S.-USSR Intermediate Nuclear Forces Treaty. This treaty has completely eliminated a class of missiles from the superpowers' arsenals, making a significant contribution to nuclear disarmament. It would be easier to ask developing countries to do something the superpowers have done already.

Option 4: Open the Debate about Nuclear Weapons

In Sweden, the economic cost of nuclear weapons was central to the decision against continuing the program. In Pakistan, cost never enters the debate, but it should.

At a seminar of the Islamabad Council of World Affairs in June 1989, participants included several members of Pakistan's national assembly and former high-ranking military officers and government officials. Also present were leading academics and members of the press. The subject was nuclear weapons. It was pointed out that India has nuclear weapons, that Pakistan therefore should have them, and that Pakistan would be safer from India if it did have them. The cost of such weapons was not considered. It is likely that many do not understand the tremendous drain on the national economy of a nuclear weapons program. The financial implications of nuclear weapons should become a part of the dialogue in Pakistan.

Nuclear weapons states such as the United States should not be the only ones to make the point of cost to the Pakistani public. European nations, Japan, and particularly countries in the capable-but-restrained category should work harder to communicate with Pakistani opinion leaders on this subject. Swedish and Japanese parliamentarians should visit their Pakistani counterparts to discuss the subject. Representatives from countries such as these would probably be more influential than would emissaries from a nuclear weapons state, who might appear to be self-serving.

Option 5: Offer Power and Prestige for Restraint

Sweden found it gained more political and moral clout by abandoning nuclear weapons than it would have by developing them. Pakistan and India could gain the clout, particularly if there were a conscious effort to make them aware of it.

Both countries should be offered a greater role in international arms control efforts, UN activities, and international fora in exchange for renouncing nuclear weapons. Similarly, the nonaligned movement, which should be seriously concerned about nuclear proliferation in its midst, could offer incentives. The nonaligned movement should curtail India's role and prestige if it continues to stonewall attempts to introduce arms control in the South Asian context.

In conclusion, the international community should make a conscious effort to examine Pakistan's and India's motivations for developing nuclear weapons and try to counter them. Export controls and attempts to get Pakistan to sign the NPT have failed. It is time for countries to negotiate with Pakistan, not only the United States, but countries that themselves have rejected nuclear weapons, countries within the region, and particularly the nonaligned nations.

Policies toward Other Proliferants

Policies mentioned above in the context of Pakistan could be applied to other potentially proliferant countries. Additionally, there may be some opportunities for policy initiatives that are region- or country-specific. For example, in the Middle East there have been a few proposals that could become the basis for a major nonproliferation breakthrough.

In April 1990, Egypt proposed a regionwide ban on weapons of mass destruction. In the past such a proposal would not have been appealing to Israel, in particular, because it possessed nuclear weapons the Arab states did not. With the spread of chemical and biological weapons capability in the region and the clear probability of nuclear capabilities,

Israel may soon find its national interests best served by considering such a proposal. Some might argue that the Arabs would also find the proposal unrealistic. Iraq, in particular, is labeled as irresponsible and intent on possessing weapons of mass destruction at any cost. Yet Iraq's foreign minister, Tareq Aziz, reportedly offered Egyptian officials just such a regional ban,[7] during a session with Arab ministers held just before Egypt announced its proposal for a regional ban.

The proposals of Egypt and Iraq may not be real, but if they are, they should not be ignored. The only way to determine their sincerity is to explore them actively.

NOTES

1. Leonard S. Spector, *The Undeclared Bomb* (Cambridge, Mass.: Ballinger, 1988), p. 121.

2. *Congressional Record,* vol. 135, no. 162, November 17, 1989 (S16103).

3. Ronald Reagan to Claiborne Pell, letter, U.S. Senate, November 18, 1988; George Bush to Claiborne Pell, letter, U.S. Senate, October 5, 1989. Author's files.

4. Bush to Pell, October 5, 1989. Author's files.

5. "U.S. Helped Persuade Pakistan to Send Troops to Saudi Arabia," *Defense & Foreign Affairs Weekly,* September 2, 1990, p. 2.; "Pakistan Sends More Troops," *London Financial Times,* September 3, 1990, p. 2.

6. Caryle Murphy, "Egypt's Foreign Minister Urges Mideast Arms Ban," *Washington Post,* April 19, 1990, p. A40.

7. Jamal Halaby, "Iraq Vows to Junk Chemical Arms If Israel Does," *Washington Times,* April 5, 1990, p. 11.

4

Chemical Weapons: Easy to Make, Hard to Detect

Chemical weapons are easy and inexpensive to manufacture and deploy. Additionally, current technology cannot detect chemical weapons production, particularly if a country tries to hide such activity. This means that any country intent on doing so can make chemical weapons, and promises to refrain from making them cannot be verified effectively.

This chapter describes the major categories of chemical weapons and their effects. It then addresses the level of difficulty each category of weapons poses to a country trying to develop its own capability to produce chemical weapons. (Chemicals intended primarily for riot control or temporary incapacitation—psychochemicals, tear gas, and vomiting agents—are not discussed.)

There are four different categories of chemical agents that have been developed to cause death or serious physical injury: choking (also referred to as respiratory), blistering (vesicants), blood (systemic), and nerve. Only chemicals that have been chosen by one or more nations for weapons use and/or stockpile are discussed here. It should be noted, however, that a variety of common chemicals can cause death or incapacitation. The December 1984 leak of methyl isocyanate from a Union Carbide factory in Bhopal, India, killed 2,500 people. Clearly, dangerous chemicals that might not make "ideal" chemical weapons could be used for that purpose, even if the original intent was for civilian applications. Thus, a variety of chemicals not developed or stockpiled as weapons could be used as such, particularly if they were available when others were not.

It is important to note that a less-developed country may not have the same standards for purity or yield as the United States. An American chemical weapons production facility should not be used as a reference for judging other countries' capacity or intent to produce chemical weapons. The United States has very high purity standards for the chemicals it uses in weapons, in part because its goal is long-term storage and high effectiveness upon use. This has posed a higher technical challenge and stricter procedures and standards for the United States. Other countries may not have such requirements.

Choking Agents

Germany first used chemical weapons in World War I against French and British troops at Ypres in April 1915.[1] More than 150 tons of chlorine gas was released from cylinders along a four-mile front, resulting in 20,000 casualties and 5,000 fatalities. Chlorine sears the lining of victims' air passages. When plasma enters the lungs from the bloodstream, victims drown in their own fluids.

In addition to chlorine, phosgene (carbonyl chloride), disphosgene (trichloromethyl chloroformate), and disulphur decafluoride have been developed as choking gases. Phosgene is more effective than chlorine because it is hydrolyzed by the water in the lining of the lungs, forming hydrochloric acid, which readily destroys the tissue.

None of the choking agents are likely to be used in a modern chemical war because their toxicity is relatively low compared to other chemical weapons. Initial irritation and smell warn of their presence, enabling gas masks to be donned before lethal exposure.[2] Additionally, they are not very persistent; in warm weather they may disperse in less than an hour, and in winter within three hours. In a "nonmodern" chemical war, however, choking agents could be quite effective. A government that chose to use a choking agent in genocide would not expect the population to be equipped with gas masks. Traces of the gas would disappear rapidly, making it unlikely that an inspection team could prove that a choking agent had been used.

If a nation were to choose to make choking agents, it would have little or no technical difficulty. The technology is World War I vintage. Making chlorine, for example, involves simple electrolysis and access to seawater. Phosgene is produced by a reaction of chlorine with carbon monoxide over charcoal in the presence of light. Chemical reactions and processes are well described in literature on the subject. Any country with experience in standard industrial chemical activity could accomplish the task.

Blistering Agents

In 1917, the Germans introduced mustard gas (sulphur mustard) delivered by shells. Mustard can be used in either liquid or vapor form. There are three major types based on the chemical formula Bis(2-chloroethyl)sulfide. There are also nitrogen mustards. In addition to causing respiratory problems that can lead to death, blistering agents cause serious eye and skin irritations, sometimes leading to blindness, vomiting, and nausea that can last for months. Blisters that form may take months to heal. Exposure is generally fatal only if the agent is inhaled. After a fatal dose, death can take days or weeks.

Even though mustard gas can penetrate regular clothing, it was not highly effective in World War I, primarily because it was delivered by shells. Spraying would have greatly increased its effectiveness. Italy proved this in 1936 when it sprayed mustard gas in Ethiopia. One of the most serious drawbacks to the user of mustard gas, however, is its persistence. If a country expects to occupy an area after clearing the enemy, mustard gas may be as much a nuisance to the occupation force as it was to the enemy.

On November 3, 1983, Iran alleged for the first time that Iraq had used chemical weapons.[3] Specialists were sent by the UN secretary-general to examine Iranian victims, take samples from the soil, and analyze unexploded bombs found at the site of alleged use. The specialists confirmed that Iraq was bombing Iranians with mustard gas. The bombs were thin steel casings containing an explosive that, when detonated, dispersed the liquid mustard as a spray and vapor. Iraq clearly proved that it was able to manufacture mustard gas as well as the bombs to disperse it. Iraq was also able to construct bombs using components from conventional weapons acquired abroad. For example, the timing fuses used on the bombs were marked in Spanish, indicating that they were imported.[4]

That Iraq was able to manufacture mustard gas is not remarkable. If Iraq were to use the Levenstein process, which involves reacting sulphur monochloride with dry ethylene, it would find the ingredients widely available because both have a number of civil uses. If Iraq were to use sodium sulfide, a less likely process, it would find this precursor chemical to be controlled by at least twenty nations. Nevertheless, sodium sulfide is manufactured in several countries that do not impose controls, including Argentina, Brazil, Colombia, Mexico, Peru, China, India, Israel, Taiwan, Bulgaria, and Poland. Sodium sulfide has many civil uses, such as in the manufacture of paper, rubber, and dyes.

Nitrogen mustards are similar to sulphur compounds, but their effects are usually more rapid. All three are less persistent than sulphur mustard. Precursors for nitrogen mustards are somewhat common and have many civil uses. Triethanolamine, for example, is a precursor for one form of nitrogen mustard. It is used in organic synthesis, detergents, cosmetics, and as a corrosion inhibitor and plasticizer. Known manufacturers are located in Australia, Austria, Brazil, Canada, China, France, Germany, Italy, Japan, Mexico, the United Kingdom, and the United States.

Lewisite is a blistering agent similar in effect to the mustards, but it results in complications due to arsenic poisoning. It causes severe eye damage within fifteen minutes of exposure and blistering within eight hours. It is rapidly destroyed by water; wet clothing affords fairly good protection.

Blood Agents

Blood agents, another legacy of World War I, are absorbed into the body primarily through inhalation. They prevent the normal utilization of oxygen by the cells and cause rapid damage to body tissues. The principal blood agents are hydrogen cyanide and cyanogen chloride. While not as lethal as a choking agent such as phosgene, they act far more quickly—causing death within fifteen minutes—and are more difficult to protect against. Special respirators must be used. Because they are so volatile, blood agents disperse very rapidly. In summer, they persist only ten minutes; in winter, an hour at most. They would be useful primarily in an area an aggressor wanted to occupy quickly. Blood agents, like the other chemical agents, are relatively easy to make. The chemical processes are well documented and widely known. No specialized equipment or experience beyond what is standard in the chemical industry would be required.

Iraq is believed by some to have used hydrogen cyanide in its war with Iran, and this was reported by the UN secretary-general's inspection team in July 1988.[5] Although victims had symptoms consistent with exposure to blood agents, if the chemical was used it dissipated from the environment so rapidly that samples from the area did not reveal its presence.

A precursor of hydrogen cyanide (as well as of some other chemical weapons agents) is sodium cyanide. It is used commercially to extract gold and silver from ores, to manufacture dyes and pigments, and to produce nylon and fumigants. It is known to be produced in Belgium, Germany, Italy, Japan, the Netherlands, South Africa, Spain, the United Kingdom, the United States, and the Soviet Union.

Nerve Agents

Nerve agents are very lethal and act rapidly, making them effective weapons in significantly smaller quantities. They are organophosphorus compounds that affect the central nervous system, primarily by inhibiting a "chemical messenger" in the body, cholinesterase. "The normal function of cholinesterase is to break down another chemical, acetylcholine, that causes muscular contraction. If the normal actions of this substance are not checked its concentration in the body will build up to danger levels, causing the muscles to go into uncontrolled spasms affecting all bodily functions."[6] The ultimate effect is respiratory paralysis and death. Nerve agents may be absorbed through the skin, digestive tract, eyes, or respiratory tract. They are liquid and generally disseminated as aerosols.

There are two main classes of nerve agents, the G-series and the V-series. The G-series includes GA (tabun, which was developed and stockpiled by the Germans in World War II), GB (sarin), GD (soman), GE, and GF. They tend to disperse more quickly than the V-series and are therefore less of a skin hazard. They are useful in battles where the territory is soon to be occupied.

V-agents are more toxic and persistent. One V-agent, for example, is about the same density as water but evaporates up to 2,000 times more slowly. V-agents are 2,000 times more toxic than mustard gas if absorbed through the skin and about 300 times more toxic if absorbed through the lungs.

Iraq recognized that nerve agents would be more effective than mustard gas, particularly in Iranian areas it wished to occupy. Iraq's use of nerve agents was reported in March 1984.[7] Mustard continued to be used in rear areas where Iraqi troops were not expected to go. Again,

Iraq proved it could manufacture not only chemical agents but also the bombs to deliver them.

Certain chemicals in nerve agents are useful for a number of civil processes. Phosphorus trichloride, for example, can be used for V- and G-agents, but it is also used in organic systhesis, insecticides, gasoline additives, platicizers, surfactants, and dyestuffs. Currently, firms that are known to make it are located in Brazil, China, Japan, India, France, Germany, Switzerland, the United Kingdom, the Soviet Union, and the United States.

Sodium fluoride, another chemical that could be used in certain G-agents and is also used in pesticides, disinfectants, dental prophylaxis, and in glass and steel manufacturing, is produced in Argentina, Belgium, China, Czechoslovakia, France, Germany, India, Israel, Italy, Japan, Mexico, and Poland.

Chemical Weapons: Hard to Detect

A system to verify that a nation does not have chemical weapons would have to be able to detect:
   • clandestine or undeclared chemical weapons stockpiles;
   • clandestine chemical weapons production facilities;
   • diversion of legitimate chemical products from commercial facilities for use in chemical weapons;
   • secret production of chemical weapons in commercial facilities;
   • stockpiling of common chemicals that could be used as chemical weapons, or their components or binary components.
Each of these is extremely difficult, some likely impossible, to detect.

A militarily significant chemical weapons stockpile can be small and easy to hide. In the future, when the United States destroys 98 percent of its chemical weapons stockpile, as it has pledged to do, any nation with even a small chemical weapons stockpile could be a threat. In early 1990, experts stated that 500 or more tons of any agent would be required for a chemical weapons conflict in Europe between NATO and Warsaw Pact troops. After the destruction of American stockpiles, 100 tons could be sufficient. One hundred tons would also be enough for a conflict outside Europe.

Finding 100 tons of a hidden chemical weapons agent in any country would be nearly impossible. The agent could be stored in containers smaller than barrels of oil and hidden in any mine, warehouse, moving railway car, or any likely or unlikely place. It would be a futile search.

Clandestine production facilities would also be very hard to detect. Quantities of weapons-usable chemicals could be produced in a small space using procedures and equipment that would have no signatures to distinguish them from a host of other chemical manufacturing activities. A small-scale chemical facility could be concealed inside a large building or built underground. Several such facilities could constitute a major production effort; production lines for various chemicals need not be located near each other. A secret facility could even be constructed to produce a militarily significant stockpile of chemical weapons and then the facility could be destroyed, leaving no sign that a weapons plant had been there.

Arms control verification experts are also concerned about chemicals that are vital to industry but are also usable in weapons. The problem they confront is that it is extremely difficult to know whether a country producing weapons-usable chemicals is doing so for weapons purposes. There are legitimate civil purposes for virtually every chemical that is a component in the known chemical weapons. (One exception is pinacolyl alcohol.) For example, Brazil, China, and India are among the countries that produce phosphorus trichloride, a chemical used in insecticides but also used in nerve gases. It would be easy for any of these nations to divert some of the phosphorus trichloride from commercial to military use without much risk of detection.

A similar problem is detecting the production of a chemical weapons agent in a commercial facility. Although highly intrusive, inspection could probably detect whether some types of chemical weapons had been produced in a particular plant, but such a finding might not be conclusive. The probability of detection is reduced in relation to the amount of agent produced; a small amount of agent would be hard to detect. Hypothetically, a nation could dedicate its chemical industry to production of chemical weapons agents for only a short time and create a militarily significant stockpile.

To avoid detection a country might also choose to stockpile the components without assembling the chemical weapons. Thus, chemicals usable as or in such weapons could be produced and stored, citing a civil purpose as the reason. In a crisis, the nation could quickly assemble and deploy the chemical weapons. Alternatively a nation could simply create a chemical weapons production capacity and, in the event of a crisis, quickly produce the weapons on the spot.

A further complication to detection is that a nation could develop a chemical weapon never produced or deployed before. New chemicals are being developed continually. Since 1957, ten million new chemicals have been recorded by the American Chemical Society's Chemical Abstracts Service.[8] If a new and unusual weapon were developed, attempts to verify its production could easily be foiled.

In summary, chemical agents are easy to make, and their production is difficult, if not impossible, to detect with currently available technology. Virtually all weapons-usable chemicals have legitimate civil uses, and the equipment and materials required for their manufacture are fairly commonplace.

NOTES

1. John Cookson and Judith Nottingham, *A Survey of Chemical and Biological Warfare* (New York: Monthly Review Press, 1969), p. 283. For a good description of chemical weapons use in World War I, see L. F. Haber, *The Poisonous Cloud* (Oxford: Clarendon Press, 1986).

2. Perry Robinson, "Chemical Weapons," in *Chemical and Biological Warfare*, ed. Steven Rose (Boston: Beacon Press, 1969), p. 21.

3. UN Security Council, "Report of the Specialists Appointed by the Secretary-General to Investigate Allegations by the Islamic Republic of Iran Concerning the Use of Chemical Weapons," S/16433, March 26, 1984, p. 1. Available from the UN Publications Office.

4. Ibid., p. 8.

5. UN Security Council, "Report of the Mission Dispatched by the Secretary-General to Investigate Allegations of the Use of Chemical Weapons in the Conflict Between the Islamic Republic of Iran and Iraq," S/20060, July 20, 1988, p. 13. Available from UN Publications Office.

6. T. J. Gander, *Nuclear, Biological, and Chemical Warfare* (New York: Hippocrene Books, 1987), p. 66.

7. UN Security Council, S/20060, p. 11.

8. *Popular Science*, June 1990, p. 22.

5

Who Has Chemical Weapons and Why

Only three countries—the United States, the Soviet Union, and Iraq—have admitted that they possess chemical weapons. However, they are not the only ones with chemical weapons programs. In February 1989, CIA director William Webster testified before the U.S. Senate that at least twenty nations can produce chemical weapons.[1] Burma, China, Egypt, Ethiopia, Indonesia, Iran, Iraq, Israel, Libya, North Korea, Syria, Taiwan, Thailand, and Vietnam are suspected of having chemical weapons programs.[2] There may be other countries with such programs too. South Korea is considered fully capable and perhaps motivated to produce chemical weapons as a deterrent to North Korea. A nation's statement that it does not possess chemical weapons is not particularly meaningful (compare the above list with Table 1).

The chemical weapons problem could readily become worse. Webster's remarks show he was talking about known chemical weapons programs in the Third World. Chemical weapons–capable nations are those with a chemical-industrial infrastructure enabling them to produce chemical weapons immediately upon a political decision to do so. By some estimates, over 100 countries now have the industrial base necessary to produce chemical weapons.[3] It is possible that in the future chemical weapons–capable nations in Europe and Japan will be faced with threats that would cause them to rethink their commitments. However, for now, the chemical weapons arms control issue is restricted to two realms: the programs of the United States and the Soviet Union, and those in the Third World.

Table 1
Nations That Have Declared They Do Not Possess Chemical Weapons

Afghanistan	Greece	Nigeria
Argentina	Guinea-Bissau	Norway
Australia	Hungary	Pakistan
Austria	Iceland	Panama
Bahrain	India	Papua New Guinea
Belgium	Indonesia	Peru
Brazil	Italy	Poland
Bulgaria	Japan	Romania
Burma	Kenya	Senegal
Canada	Korea, North	South Africa
Chile	Korea, South	Sudan
China	Kuwait	Sweden
Cook Islands	Libya	Switzerland
Cyprus	Madagascar	Tanzania
Czechoslovakia	Malaysia	Thailand
Denmark	Malta	Togo
Egypt	Mexico	Turkey
Ethiopia	Mongolia	Uganda
Finland	Morocco	United Kingdom
FR Germany	Netherlands	Venezuela
France	New Zealand	Vietnam
German DR	Nicaragua	Yugoslavia

The United States and the Soviet Union

During and after World War II, the United States produced chemical weapons and openly acknowledged doing so. Then, for eighteen years, from 1969 to 1987, the United States did not produce chemical weapons. The United States again halted production in spring 1990.

The Soviet Union also produced chemical weapons during and after World War II, although it did not admit possessing them until 1987. During the 1980s, the United States became increasingly worried about Soviet chemical weapons capabilities for a variety of reasons. First and foremost was the fact that Soviet chemical weaponry was newer and greater in quantity. Additionally, there was and is a serious imbalance in overall chemical weapons preparedness of the two superpowers. As

Table 2
Chemical Weapons Preparedness of
the United States and the Soviet Union, 1989

	U.S.	USSR
Personnel dedicated to chemical weapons	8,500	80,000
Training battalions	1	19
Military chemical weapons schools	1	4
Length of longest course	6 months	5 years
Field training areas	1	78
Mobile decontamination devices	1,000	30,000

Source: U.S. Department of Defense, "Chemical Warfare—A Real and Growing Threat,"
p. 8. Used by permission.

Table 2 shows, Soviet attention to and preparedness for chemical
warfare greatly exceeds that of the United States.

In contrast to the Soviet arsenal, American chemical weaponry is
outmoded. While Soviet chemical weapons forces were being modernized,
the aging U.S. stockpile physically deteriorated, and a few of the oldest
weapons began to leak. Military effectiveness of U.S. chemical weapons
declined as the intended delivery systems were retired from the inventory.
By 1989, only 10 percent of the U.S. chemical weapons stockpile was
estimated to be usable and effective.[4]

The Reagan administration decided to destroy the old, increasingly
dangerous weapons and to modernize chemical weapons capability to
make the weapons more safe and secure. It chose to produce binary
weapons—two chemicals that, when separate, are not lethal but when
mixed become a weapon.

As of mid-1990, the United States is estimated to have a chemical
weapons stockpile of 30,000 tons. The Soviet Union says it has 50,000
tons. U.S. intelligence estimates of the Soviet stockpile have varied
widely up to 300,000 tons. There is currently no technical means for
any nation to verify the size of another's stockpile.

Iraq and Iran

The use of chemical weapons by Iran and Iraq in their war was well
documented. Iraq has admitted to possessing chemical weapons and

has threatened to use them again. "We do not need an atomic bomb," said Iraqi leader Saddam Hussein on April 2, 1990. "We have the dual chemical. Whoever threatens us with the atomic bomb, we will annihilate him with the dual chemical."[5] The phrase "dual chemical" may refer to the fact that Iraq not only developed mustard gas, a blistering agent, but also one or more nerve agents. "Dual chemical" might also refer to binary weapons such as those designed by the United States for safety purposes.

The Iran-Iraq war is important to the issue of chemical weapons proliferation for two primary reasons. First, it eroded the taboo against chemical weapons. Second, it was widely perceived to have saved Iraq from defeat in the war. Chemical weapons were used without international punishment and were militarily effective; this created good advertisement for chemical weapons proliferation.

Iraq first began to use chemical weapons on a limited scale in 1983. UN inspections teams subsequently found evidence of Iraqi use of mustard gas and an organophosphorous compound, probably the nerve agent GA. Iraq had produced the agents domestically and by 1988 had an estimated annual capability of 700 tons.[6] Other estimates of Iraq's chemical weapons production have ranged even higher.[7] It has at least three plants to produce agents, all modified pesticide plants built with the help of Western European companies.[8]

German prosecutors have developed evidence that West German companies were engaged in helping Iraq weaponize its chemical plants as well. Water Engineering Trading G.m.b.H., for example, is accused of knowingly providing Iraq with machinery to convert 122mm rockets and rocket-propelled grenades into chemical weapons delivery systems.[9]

Iraq is continuing to expand its production capabilities not only because it wants a larger stockpile but also to assure its own supply of component chemicals. A large $2.5 billion petrochemical complex is being built at Musayyib, south of Baghdad. It is expected to become operational in 1994 and will be able to produce enough thiodyglycol to manufacture 1,000 tons of mustard gas.[10]

Advanced countries are not the only sources of important relevant supplies. In March 1989, an Indian official admitted that an Indian trading firm sold thionyl chloride, a precursor chemical for mustard gas, to Iran. The circuitous route by which the chemical was obtained is a typical ploy to mask such sales. A West German company, Rheineisen Chemical Products, contracted with the Indian State Trading Corporation for $50,000 worth of the chemical. The trading company then bought the chemical from Transpek Private, based in Bombay. Rather than send the chemical directly to Iran, which might have attracted attention, it was sent to Dubai and then transferred to Iran.[11]

Although a subsequent shipment of thionyl chloride from India to Iran was stopped,[12] it is not certain how much of the chemical Iran and other countries have purchased from India overall. Transpek Private, one of the manufacturers of thionyl chloride in India, increased its production from 150 tons in 1979 to 2,203 tons in 1987. Company officials admitted that several hundred tons were exported in 1988.[13] Indian companies reportedly also sold chemicals to Iraq and Egypt.[14]

Western European companies also reportedly have sold chemical weapons–related technology to Iran. The West German company Bayer sold Iran equipment usable in chemical weapons production.[15] Imported in 1987, the equipment was installed in the Ghasvine Chemical Complex, a plant Iran originally claimed would be used for phosphate-based pesticide production.

A British company is said to have a contract with Iran for a $37 million pesticide plant that would use phosphorus pentasulfide, a chemical ingredient in two nerve agents.[16] Again, the acquisition attempt was covered up; Iran approached a Dutch subsidiary of the British company rather than go directly to its central offices.

Libya

Information about Libya's chemical weapons facility at Rabta, about fifty miles south of Tripoli, was made publicly available in late 1988, when the U.S. government decided to declassify and release certain intelligence information. The U.S. motive was to persuade West German companies to end their participation in the project and to familiarize the public with the threat Rabta posed.

In 1984, West German companies sold Libya a complete facility capable of manufacturing chemical weapons. The transaction was obscured by first exporting the chemical equipment to Hong Kong and then forwarding it to Libya. The West German government sentenced the head of the chemical firm Imhausen-Chemie to five years in prison for his role in the planning and construction of the $50 million Rabta facility. A West German investigation revealed that German companies sent not only documents on production but instrumentation and equipment for the site.[17] The investigation also concluded, as did U.S. intelligence, that the facility was solely intended for producing chemical weapons. Although Libya has repeatedly declared that Rabta is a pharmaceutical manufacturing plant, it is used to produce mustard and nerve agents. The facility is surrounded by fences, has heavy security, and is protected with North Korean surface-to-air missiles.[18]

Production of chemical weapons began at Rabta perhaps as early as 1987 and continued into 1988. An accident reportedly shut down production in early 1988, and the Libyans had difficulty restarting the plant. Production was low and intermittent due to technical problems and, perhaps, international political pressures. Rabta had some difficulty obtaining adequate water supplies and may have had problems getting precursor chemicals. It probably did not reach full-scale continuous operation until early 1990, although it could have been producing chemical weapons since mid-1989. Figures vary, but reports in early 1990 indicated that Libya had produced thirty tons,[19] or perhaps fifty metric tons,[20] since mid-1989.

On March 14, 1990, a fire was reported at the Rabta facility. It was initially claimed to be sabotage but later determined to be a ruse. If indeed Libya ever does have a significant accident at Rabta, repairs will almost certainly require foreign assistance and equipment. Although Libya has had access to foreign help in designing, building, and maintaining Rabta, the notoriety of the facility is likely to deter Western firms from assisting in any needed repairs. On-site foreign laborers, including some from Pakistan and Thailand, are unlikely to be skilled enough to help. China, however, might be of help, having reportedly assisted Libya with weaponization. Additionally, the U.S. State Department expressed concern in May 1990 that China had supplied Libya with chemicals for weapons.[21] Libya is likely to use chemical weapons in one of its many confrontations; in fact, Libya is widely believed to have used chemical weapons against Chad in 1987.

Other Programs

Less information is made available to the public about other chemical weapons programs. Two countries believed to be engaged in such programs, but whose activities are cloaked in secrecy, are Egypt and Syria.

Egypt's expeditionary forces used imported chemical weapons against royalist forces in Yemen during that country's 1962–69 civil war.[22] Egypt's efforts to develop its own chemical weapons production capability were boosted in 1986 when it struck a deal with Krebs AG, a Zurich-based company, to deliver key components of a plant to produce the nerve agent Sarin.[23] Although the Swiss government was notified about the sale, its export control laws were insufficiently strict to stop the fulfillment of the contract. The same company has been involved in the sale of similar plants (to make pharmaceuticals and pesticides) to Iran.

Even less information is available about Syria's efforts. According to Israeli information, a military research institute north of Damascus, code-named Sers, is preparing a new chemical weapons warhead for Syria's Scud ballistic missiles.[24] There is insufficient data to provide a fuller description, however.

Why Possess Chemical Weapons?

There are two reasons why a nation would want to possess chemical weapons. The first is to gain military superiority. Iraq knew that Iran did not have chemical weapons nor defenses against them. Baghdad built and used mustard and nerve gas weapons to gain a military advantage. It worked.

If Iraqi chemical weapons use began in 1983, and perhaps as early as 1981, how can it be said that such weapons were crucial to the ultimate victory of Iraq in 1987? The answer is clear in Iranian chemical casualty figures (see Figure 1). It took some time for Iraq to fully weaponize its chemical weapons agent and perfect its delivery capabilities. By 1986, Iraq had begun to employ chemical weapons more extensively and effectively. Iranian chemical casualities mounted. Word of the horrors of chemical weapons spread, and Iranian troops proved inept and ill-trained in using protective gear. Even though three out of four chemical casualties recovered by Iran had used a gas mask, injuries were severe, often fatal. Iran signed a ceasefire in August 1988.

Other less developed countries noted Iraq's successes—both the ease of acquiring such lethal weapons without a sophisticated infrastructure and the use of them to military advantage. This has set the stage for a host of other countries to consider chemical weapons production.

The second major motive for acquiring chemical weapons is deterrence. Deterrence is based on the fear that a perceived enemy constitutes a threat that can and should be countered. History has several examples that demonstrate chemical weapons deterrence works. In World War I,

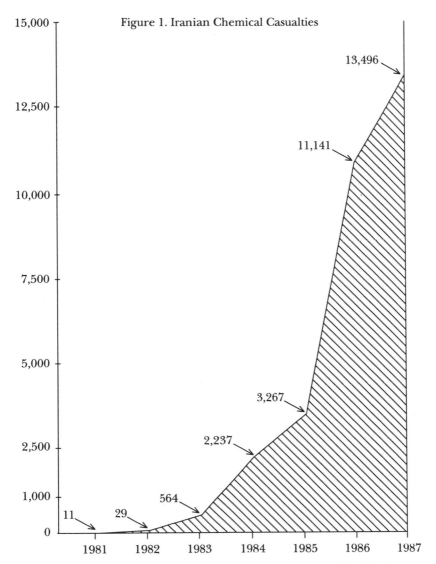

Figure 1. Iranian Chemical Casualties

Redrawn from Lee Waters, "Chemical Weapons in the Iran-Iraq War,"
Military Review, October 1990, p. 58. Used by permission.

before the Allies had deployed chemical weapons, Germany had such
weapons and used them. Then the Allies got chemical weapons. In
World War II, both sides possessed chemical weapons but realized
how horrible their use would be and refrained. Historically, chemical
weapons have been used when only one party to a conflict has them:

Italy against Ethiopia in 1935; Japan against China starting in 1937; Egypt against Yemen in the 1960s; Iraq against Iran starting in 1983; Libya against Chad in 1987.

A primary problem with deterrence is that it can actually promote the acquisition of chemical weapons by nations that otherwise might not acquire them. Iran is the most recent example of this. Although Iran may have developed chemical weapons anyway, it is certain that Iraq's possession and use of chemical weapons caused Iran to build them too.

As outlined above, chemical weapons are viewed as being a deterrent against a perceived enemy's chemical weapons. Additionally, some nations view chemical weapons as a deterrent against other weapons of mass destruction as well. At the Paris Conference on Chemical Weapons Use in January 1989, several Arab states, supported by other developing countries' representatives, argued that chemical weapons cannot be banned in the Middle East without nuclear weapons also being eliminated.[25] Iraq, Syria, Egypt, and Libya are among those that have taken the position that an Arab chemical weapons capability is necessary to counter Israel's nuclear capability.

In conclusion, there are a variety of chemical weapons programs, most of which are in the less-developed countries. Some are undoubtedly motivated by regimes seeking military advantage over adversaries. However, some are intended as a deterrent. As the number of countries in possession of chemical weapons increases, it will very likely snowball, as neighboring countries seek to protect themselves with a chemical weapons capability of their own.

NOTES

1. Michael R. Gordon, "CIA Sees a Developing World with Developed Arms," *New York Times International,* February 10, 1989.

2. Stephen Engelberg, "Chemical Arms: Third World Trend," *New York Times,* January 7, 1989, p. 5.

3. Robin Wright, "Chemical Arms: Old and Deadly Scourge Returns," *Los Angeles Times,* October 9, 1988, p. 1.

4. U.S. Department of Defense, "Chemical Warfare—A Real and Growing Threat," May 1989, p. 8. Author's files.

5. Alan Cowell, "Iraq Chief, Boasting of Poison Gas, Warns of Disaster If Israelis Strike," *New York Times,* April 3, 1990, p. 1.

6. Yossef Bodansky and Vaughn S. Forrest, "Chemical Weapons in the

Third World: Iraq's Expanding Chemical Arsenal," (U.S. House of Representatives Task Force on Terrorism and Unconventional Warfare, May 29, 1990), p. 10. Available from U.S. Government Printing Office.

7. Robert Pear, "Iraq Can Deliver, U.S. Chemical Arms Experts Say," *New York Times,* April 3, 1990, p. 8.

8. One report estimates Iraq can produce 5,000 tons of nerve gas per year. See Kenneth R. Timmerman, *The Poison Gas Connection,* (Los Angeles: Simon Wiesenthal Center, 1990) and "Chemical Warfare: Ban the World's Machine Guns," *The Economist,* June 4, 1988, p. 22.

9. Frederick Kempe, "Two Germans Say Firms Made Iraqi Arms Sales," *Wall Street Journal,* October 10, 1990, p. 14.

10. James Dorsey, "Iraq Hunting Cash for Mustard-Gas Plant," *Washington Times,* April 27, 1990, p. 8.

11. Sanjoy Hazarika, "India Says It Sold Iran a Chemical Used in Poison Gas," *New York Times,* July 1, 1989, p. 1.

12. "India Halts a Shipment of Chemicals for Iran," *New York Times,* July 6, 1989, p. 3.

13. Stephen Engelberg and Michael R. Gordon, "India Seen as Key on Chemical Arms," *New York Times,* July 10, 1989, p. 1.

14. Ibid.

15. "Bonn Probes Firm's Sale of Gas Chemicals to Iran," *Washington Times,* January 12, 1990, p. 9.

16. Ian Mather and Sebastian Grant, "U.S. Halts British Firm's Nerve Gas Plant Deal in Iran," *London Sunday Telegraph,* February 4, 1990, p. 12.

17. "West German Charged in Libyan Gas Affair," *Washington Post,* March 23, 1990, p. A 18.

18. Paul Bedard, "Libya Making Nerve Gas," *Washington Times,* March 8, 1990, p. 1.

19. Michael R. Gordon, "U.S.-Bonn Split on Libya Is Seen," *New York Times,* March 8, 1990, p. 17.

20. "Libya Denies Latest Chemical Arms Charge," *Washington Times,* March 9, 1990, p. 2.

21. David Hoffman and Lena H. Sun, "U.S. Tells China of Concern Over Report of Aid to Libya," *Washington Post,* June 7, 1990, p. 34.

22. William Claiborne, "Egypt's Army Experienced in Waging Chemical Warfare," *Washington Post,* August 17, 1990, p. A18.

23. Michael R. Gordon and Stephen Engelberg, "Egypt Accused of Big Advance on Poison Gas," *New York Times,* March 10, 1989, p. 1.

24. Jill Smolowe, "Return of the Silent Killer," *Time,* August 22, 1988, p. 48.

25. James M. Markham, "Arabs Link Curbs on Gas and A–Arms," *New York Times,* January 9, 1989, p. 8.

6

Policies to Control Chemical Weapons

Like its policies to combat the spread of nuclear weapons, America's chemical weapons nonproliferation policies attempt to either limit the supply of or demand for chemical weapons. Those that attempt to limit the supply of materials, equipment, and know-how also limit the ability of nations to develop chemical weapons by restricting their technical capabilities. Policies that attempt to lessen the demand for chemical weapons—either by reducing incentives for acquiring them or by building political barriers to doing so—dampen or eliminate the motivations of nations to develop chemical weapons.

In addition to these policies, the United States has undertaken extensive chemical weapons arms control efforts in its bilateral relationship with the Soviet Union that complement and reinforce nonproliferation policies. This chapter addresses these three types of arms control policies.

Policies to Limit Supply

The dominant method of limiting supply is export control. The United States is the primary proponent of export controls, and it uses them to limit both exports to specific countries and exports of certain chemicals. Currently, the United States has two export control regulations that cover the sale of chemical weapons–related items: the Export Administration Regulations (EAR), and International Traffic in Arms Regulations (ITAR). The EAR, issued and administered by the U.S. Department of Commerce, apply the following controls:

- A license is required for export of nine "core list" chemicals to all destinations except NATO member countries, Australia, Austria, Ireland, Japan, New Zealand, and Switzerland;

• Forty-one "warning list" chemicals are controlled so that they will not be exported to Iran, Iraq, Syria, Libya, or any embargoed country;

• All chemicals subject to foreign policy–based controls will require a license prohibiting reexport to Iran, Iraq, Syria, and Libya. The reexport requirement does not apply to reexports from or to NATO members, Australia, Austria, New Zealand, Ireland, Japan, or Switzerland.

The ITAR are administered by the Department of State, which decides whether a license may be given for export of any item on a munitions control list. The list contains items that are directly military in nature: chemical agents with military application; equipment for the dissemination, detection of, identification of, and defense against chemical agents; and technical data directly related to the above, including production of chemical agents.

The EAR limit the export of component chemicals and targets specific countries. The ITAR restrict the flow of chemical weapons agents, as well as equipment that can be used to make chemical weapons. For example, the ITAR require licensing before export of chemical process equipment with linings suitable for handling highly corrosive chemicals (i.e., equipment with glass, Teflon, or plastic lining), scrubber units for ventilation systems, waste treatment supplies, and a host of related hardware.

In addition to tight domestic controls on chemical weapons–related exports, the United States has sought to internationalize its export control criteria and methods. The Australia Group, an informal voluntary forum of industrialized nations formed in 1984, is the primary vehicle for these efforts. This twenty-member group includes Australia, Austria, Canada, Japan, New Zealand, Norway, Switzerland, the United States, and European Community member countries. Representatives of these countries meet periodically and regularly use diplomatic channels to exchange information on chemical weapons proliferation problems. In particular, they attempt to coordinate export controls on fifty chemicals and work to inform their respective chemical industries to avoid transactions that might contribute to proliferation.

The United States also uses bilateral relations to urge other countries to be cautious in exporting chemicals and related technology. For example, representatives of the United States and the Soviet Union have met several times to discuss measures to restrain chemical weapons proliferation.

Problems with Supply Limitation Policies

Export controls cannot prevent proliferation and may not even slow it. There are at least four good reasons why. First, while some chemical weapons agents are complex, others can be made with technology that is simple and readily available. The requirements for producing most agents are no more demanding than many chemical-industrial activities. Journals and books list formulas and describe the production processes for many agents, and standard chemical industry practices are applicable.

Second, export controls fail because most precursor chemicals and weapons-related equipment are applicable to civil or weapons uses. Phosphorus oxychloride, for example, is a chemical used in tabun, a nerve agent, and in a variety of legitimate chemical industry processes and products including organic synthesis, plasticizers, gasoline additives, hydraulic fluids, insecticides, semiconductor-grade silicon, and flame retardants. Thionyl chloride is another component for a host of chemical weapons agents (three nerve agents, two types of sulphur mustard, and all three nitrogen mustards) that has civil uses in organic synthesis, chlorinating agents, pesticides, and plastics.

Equipment that is useful for chemical weapons production, vats, piping, and other process equipment, is also useful in manufacturing pharmaceuticals. Denying export of such equipment is difficult when moral arguments can be made for its use in producing medicines. Likewise, there are the legitimate needs of chemical industries in the developing world—for producing pesticides and fertilizer. Such a civil plant, depending on how it was designed, could be turned to producing chemical weapons agents in days or even hours.

A third major weakness of chemical weapons export controls is the large number of potential suppliers of chemicals and processing equipment. A sophisticated infrastructure is not required for the manufacture of chemical weapons components. In fact, the application of export controls by Western industrialized states is likely to stimulate the development of alternative suppliers. Chemical companies—particularly in countries that are poor and/or have insufficient control over local industry—will recognize that there is hard currency to be made from chemical exports and will thus manufacture them. As mentioned in the previous chapter, India is a case in point. It has exported at least one chemical to Iran and perhaps to other nations.

In the future, export controls will likely become futile because of a fourth problem: countries will increasingly be able to make their own chemical weapons agents. Iraq provides a good example. It was planning to process its own crude oil in a petrochemical plant under construction at Musayyib, south of Baghdad.[1] The refined petroleum would be turned into widely used chemicals, ethylene and its derivatives. One related product would be ethylene oxide, which is used to make antifreeze for automobiles. It is also needed to make thiodyglycol, a precursor of mustard gas. Iraq would no longer have needed to rely on imports and could have itself become a supplier. In fact, Iraq had been rumored to have provided chemical weapons to its ally, Sudan.[2] With the Gulf War, it is very likely that the Musayyib facility was damaged or destroyed.

The United States has recognized that export controls cannot stop proliferation. A Department of Commerce report to Congress on chemical export controls explains: "The purpose of these controls is to prevent American contribution to, and thereby to distance the United States from, the proliferation and illegal use of chemical weapons. These controls demonstrate continued US opposition to increasing proliferation by terrorist and aggressor nations."[3] No claim is made that export controls will stop proliferation; rather, the controls are meant to make sure U.S.-origin chemicals are not used in the process and to symbolize U.S. opposition to chemical weapons proliferation.

Some have argued that export controls will not cause any harm and may do some good. On the contrary, as noted above, export controls stimulate the development of alternative suppliers who are less fastidious. Even worse, export controls create the impression of a solution and thereby distract attention from potentially more productive policy alternatives.

Although it is clearly unacceptable politically to advocate removing export controls on weapons-related chemicals, equipment, and technology, such controls should not be the centerpiece of America's or any other nation's chemical weapons nonproliferation policy. Excessive focus on export controls distracts precious diplomatic and bureaucratic attention from the policies more likely to be successful in addressing the spread of chemical weapons.

Policies to Limit Demand

Policies to limit demand focus on reducing incentives for acquiring chemical weapons or on building political barriers to doing so. The Hague Convention of 1899 was a political barrier. It outlawed chemical warfare, declaring, "The contracting powers agree to abstain from the use of projectiles, the sole object of which is the diffusion of asphyxiating or deleterious gases." In 1907, the Second Hague Convention added, "It is especially forbidden to employ poison or poisoned weapons." Germany, a signatory of both conventions, was the first to use chemical weapons in World War I. Other nations, also parties to the conventions, followed suit.

Revulsion against the use of chemical weapons was so strong that, following the Great War, efforts to eliminate chemical weaponry were reinitiated. This led to the Geneva Protocol of 1925, which prohibits the use of asphyxiating, poisonous, or other gases in warfare. Like the Hague conventions, there was no means to enforce the Geneva agreement. Nevertheless, the prohibition was fairly effective. During World War II, the Allies and Germany announced that the protocol would be respected. Chemical weapons were almost absent from the battlefield. Exceptions were Japan's use in China, Italy's use in Ethiopia, and Germany's use in concentration camps.

Since World War II there have been a number of allegations that chemical weapons have been used. This renewed the criticism of the Geneva Protocol, the weakness of which mirrored the problems of the Hague conventions and led the UN Conference on Disarmament to develop a broader convention. The UN has tried for the past two decades to generate an agreement that, in addition to a ban on use, would ban the development, production, stockpiling, and transfer of chemical weapons. Several problems have plagued these negotiations. One of the most important has been the lack of agreement on verification. A central question has been what to do about undeclared facilities— places where a nation might produce or store chemical weapons without acknowledging it.

Negotiations in Geneva were given new impetus in 1983, when Iraq began to use chemical weapons in its war with Iran. In 1984, Vice President Bush presented the Conference on Disarmament with a draft treaty for a chemical weapons ban. It contained a significant proposal on verification providing for inspection anywhere or anytime a violation was suspected.

Despite the U.S. initiative, the Geneva negotiations remained tied in knots. Even though the "anywhere, anytime" provision was attractive, it was and is considered by many experts on verification to be inadequate, providing little assurance that a country is not cheating. In addition to continuing troubles with verification, there was no decision on key questions such as what constitutes chemical weapons or how bureaucratic organizations to administer the ban would be structured and staffed.

Problems with the Chemical Weapons Ban

Although there are disagreements—likely solvable—about how a chemical weapons treaty should read, there are three very serious problems that may prove impossible to solve. The first is that it is unlikely that a treaty can be effectively verified with today's technology. The second is that many potential proliferants are unlikely to sign the treaty. The third is the absence of credible sanctions to deter and punish users of chemical weapons.

Verification is needed for determination of the size, location, and composition of a nation's stockpile; proof of destruction; and assurance about possible nondeclared chemical weapons production capability. The greatest progress has been made in verifying the destruction of chemical weapons. "The problems lie in detecting hidden stockpiles (a surprisingly small amount of chemical weapons are regarded as militarily significant); guarding against rapid conversion of benign chemical production plants into chemical weapons production; and preventing development and clandestine weaponization of exotic poisons on the margin between chemistry and biology."[4] There are also problems with verifying that there are no covert chemical weapons facilities.

Verifying nonproduction in known facilities will require very intrusive measures. This is objectionable to U.S. companies for constitutional as well as proprietary reasons. The Fourth Amendment guarantees against unreasonable searches and seizures. This would directly conflict with "anywhere, anytime" inspections. High-technology U.S. chemical companies fear that secret formulas will be stolen and that verification inspections may amount to industrial espionage.

Intrusive inspection is likely to be objectionable for practical and economic reasons as well. To determine that a facility has not been used to produce nerve agents, for example, may require inspecting gaskets, removing and testing pipes, and a host of costly activities. If this were required of the many facilities in many nations—as many as 10,000 worldwide—it could prove to be too much effort for such uncertain results. One estimate by an expert at the Los Alamos National Laboratory set the costs of verifying a chemical weapons global ban at several hundred million dollars per year.[5]

Despite experimentation in the commercial chemical industry and much negotiation at the Geneva conference, there is no consensus about verification. Also, there is no provision for financing verification activities, which would undoubtedly be very expensive. Poorer nations, particularly those without or with only a few chemical-industrial facilities, are unlikely to want to pay for such expensive undertakings.

A global ban on chemical weapons may not prove easy to achieve. The inadequacy of verification measures is one of the primary reasons why developing countries would not agree to it. As one Latin American representative at the Conference on Disarmament in Geneva asked, "What is to be done about verifying destruction of chemical weapons in countries that do not acknowledge having them?" He opined that his government, although represented at the conference, would not adhere to a ban because neighboring countries soon were likely to become chemical weapons producers. Another less-developed country at the conference raised a different objection to a global ban: "Why should countries which are not represented at the Conference on Disarmament agree to sign a treaty that they were not involved in negotiating?" The conference is limited to forty nations plus an unlimited number of nonvoting observers.

The United States has tried to focus attention on the proliferation problem, but with little success. During the Paris Conference on Chemical Weapons Use, held January 7–11, 1989, the United States raised the issue of proliferation. Less-developed countries rejected attempts to address the problem in any concrete way, saying that they would not give up the chemical weapons option until the problem of nuclear proliferation had been solved. The Paris conference reaffirmed the aims of the Geneva Protocol and focused worldwide attention on the problems posed by chemical weapons. But no concrete suggestions or actions resulted.

In September 1989, another international conference was held, this time in Canberra, Australia. The worldwide chemical manufacturing industry discussed how companies could help prevent proliferation, primarily through a cautious approach to exporting. Prior to this conference, the United States once again proposed that proliferation be discussed. The reaction was swift. Third-world countries threatened to boycott the conference, and Australia, worried that the conference would fail if these nations did not attend, obtained U.S. agreement to downplay the proliferation issue.

Neither the Paris nor the Canberra conference addressed the problems of verification or proliferation. One outcome, however, was to raise public expectations of progress toward a global ban. This has stimulated discussion in the United States as to whether a ban would be worthwhile even if it were not effectively verifiable. The answer is that it might be, were it not for the fact that sanctions against violators, too, seem to be failing. Without verification or sanctions, a global ban would be even less effective than the Geneva Protocol because deterrence would not be possible.

U.S.-USSR Chemical Weapons Arms Control

Despite the slow pace of the Geneva multilateral negotiations on a chemical weapons ban, the United States and the Soviet Union have made rapid progress toward controlling chemical weapons bilaterally. Initially, bilateral agreements centered on destruction of a large proportion of the superpowers' respective stockpiles.

In Wyoming during a September 1989 meeting between U.S. Secretary of State James Baker and Soviet Foreign Minister Eduard Schevardnadze, a plan was devised for each country to reveal the size of its chemical weapons stockpile and determine how destruction would take place. Both sides agreed to a two-phase bilateral verification experiment and data exchange. Phase one required each side to disclose the size and composition of its chemical weapons stockpile as well as the location of production, storage, and destruction facilities. It also called for mutual "familiarization visits" to one another's weapons-related facilities. No reference was made to the possibility that either country might not declare some sites, and no provisions were made for such event.

The second phase of what is known as the Wyoming Agreement provided for more detailed information and a limited number of challenge on-site inspections. By including such challenge inspections—to be carried out when one party is suspicious of the activities or nature of a site in the other country—it was hoped that the likelihood of cheating would be reduced. The second phase would begin within four months of when a chemical weapons treaty is likely to be initialled.[6]

On September 25, 1989, President Bush initiated further progress toward a global ban. In his address before the United Nations, he proposed that the United States and the Soviet Union agree to cut their chemical arsenals to an interim level equal to 20 percent of the current U.S. stockpile. He stated that the United States would destroy 98 percent of its chemical weapons within eight years of signing the Geneva treaty if the Soviet Union would also sign the agreement. The Soviets agreed, contingent on both sides stopping chemical weapons production.

Bilateral talks, centering on the Bush proposals, were put on a fast track in anticipation of the May 1990 summit between Presidents Bush and Gorbachev. At the summit, the two leaders signed an executive agreement that stated that some arms control steps be taken initially and that others be taken when "sufficient participation" in a global treaty is achieved. Their agreement states that the United States and the Soviet Union will cease chemical weapons production and will cut their arsenals to 5,000 metric tons of chemical weapons agent by no later than December 31, 2002. The destruction must begin by the end of 1992. Upon entry into force of a multilateral treaty banning chemical weapons, U.S. and Soviet stockpiles must be further reduced to a level no greater than 500 tons within eight years. At that time, a conference of states party to the multilateral treaty will determine whether participation in the ban is sufficient to call for destroying the remainder of the U.S. and Soviet stockpiles. A key criterion for the United States will be whether all chemical weapons–capable nations have adhered to the global ban.

Problems with the Bilateral Agreement

Verification, already discussed, is a serious problem for chemical weapons arms control. The size of the declared stockpiles cannot be confirmed, so secret stores are possible. Existence of clandestine production capabilities cannot be detected. Easiest to verify is the destruction of declared stockpiles.

Destroying thousands of tons of chemical weapons will be a monumental and costly task. U.S. experiences to date in trying to destroy some of its stockpile provides an example. In 1985, Congress passed Public Law 99-145, which directed the Department of Defense to destroy old U.S. unitary chemical weapons. All disposal was to take place by September 30, 1994. However, in 1988 this deadline was extended to 1997 after some of the complex technical steps involved in the task were better understood. Even this deadline is unlikely to be met.

The first disposal site was built on Johnston Atoll, approximately 700 miles southwest of Hawaii, at a cost of approximately $240 million. It had explosion-resistant bunkers and a remote-controlled incinerator that burned chemical weapons components at 2,700° F. The processes used have been under development since 1972 and under experimentation in a pilot-scale facility in Utah since 1979. In addition to the Johnston Atoll site, eight destruction facilities will be built in the United States. Multiple destruction facilities, although more expensive than a single central site, will be used to minimize movement of chemical weapons across populated areas en route to destruction.

Between 1985 and 1990, the planning and construction of the nine facilities cost $1.1 billion.[7] In 1990, an additional $430 million was requested. It is expected that an additional $3 billion at least will be needed to complete the project.

Aside from financial and technical difficulties, environmental groups and the public have had some serious concerns. Federal agencies—the Environmental Protection Agency, the Department of Labor, the Occupational Safety and Health Administration, the Department of Health and Human Services, and the Federal Emergency Management Agency—have levied requirements and been intensively involved in planning and executing the projects.

U.S. destruction of chemical weapons stockpiles is likely to succeed, although not at original estimates of cost and timing. The possibilities for Soviet chemical weapons destruction are a very different story, however. As of mid-1990, the Soviet Union has not even begun to prepare for elimination. It has no developed technology and probably has not sufficiently budgeted for the effort. The first Soviet site at Chapayevsk, 550 miles southwest of Moscow, was closed before operation due to public outcry over environmental concerns.

To solve some of the chemical weapons destruction problems, the Soviet Union has turned to the United States. Although the United States is willing to help, there are reasons why it is hesitant. Can the United States be sure that its processes are right for Soviet circumstances? If the Soviets were to be sloppy in applying U.S. technology and caused a disaster, what would the implications be? Who would pay for the costly, first-class facility designs to be used? Additionally, the Soviet Union is inclined to use a different process that would first neutralize the chemical weapons. While less risky in the short run, this method produces a more hazardous waste ash. This is a long-term problem that the United States chose to avoid with its high-technology processing.

Despite the troubles faced by the chemical weapons destruction agreement, it represents the greatest achievements thus far on chemical arms control. Now there is need for additional policies to address the proliferation problem and the steps to take in the event of chemical weapons use or violation of arms control measures.

Additional Policies

Two of the most commonly discussed options for dealing with chemical weapons use are assistance to those attacked and sanctions against the user. In the case of the former, the types of assistance that might be given vary but could include protective gear, decontamination equipment, and medical assistance. These will do little good, however, if the user has already won the war with chemical weapons. Assistance to the attacked might also entail military help, but, again, the war could be over before such aid arrived.

Promises of assistance are not likely to dampen the desires of a nation wanting a chemical weapons deterrent. During Iran's war with Iraq, Iranians acquired gas masks and received substantial international medical assistance. As a result, the severity of injuries was greatly reduced in many cases, as was documented in reports to the UN secretary-general.[8] Nevertheless, injuries were sustained and the environment was seriously contaminated; and Iran developed its own chemical weapons as a deterrent. Thus, promises of military assistance against chemical weapons use are probably not a viable solution. Few, if any, nations would have aided Iran militarily—for political or economic reasons—even though it was the victim of chemical weapons attacks.

If verification is not effective and there are no technical obstacles to prevent a nation from seeking a deterrent, perhaps disincentives offer the best alternative. Although sanctions historically do not have a very good track record, they are perhaps the policy most likely to succeed, particularly if widespread international commitment to sanctions could be obtained.

In September 1988, President François Mitterrand of France urged the UN to endorse an international embargo of products, technologies, and weapons against any nation using chemical weapons. Historically, the effectiveness of sanctions—particularly embargoes—has been dependent mainly on the breadth of participation in the sanctions and the depth of their application. If widespread commitment to an embargo were obtained and documented, it would probably act as an influential deterrent to the use of chemical weapons by nations.

One of the key objections to the Mitterrand proposal at the time it was made was the fact that chemical weapons use was difficult to determine. In 1988, for example, after the United States accused Iraq of using chemical weapons against its Kurdish minority, the UN was unable to conduct an inspection. Neither Turkey nor Iraq would allow the UN team to examine Kurds. Even if the team had gained admittance, the procedures and readiness of inspectors were inadequate to determine whether chemical agents might have been used and already dissipated.

Subsequently, the UN secretary-general prepared guidelines and procedures for investigating reports of possible chemical weapons use. These procedures recommend that UN member states allow a UN team to enter any territory where there was allegation of chemical weapons use. A nation may still deny entry, but there is now a mechanism for determining the facts endorsed by the UN General Assembly. If the mechanism works, determining whether chemical weapons has been used becomes credible and clears the way for implementation of the Mitterrand proposal. The UN could proceed to develop international guidelines for immediate, universal, nonoptional sanctions in any proven case of chemical weapons use or when UN teams are not allowed to inspect for alleged use.

Aside from assistance to an attacked nation or international sanctions, there are few if any politically attractive policy options. One possibility that should be discussed is minimal reserved stockpiles, an idea proposed by France that was unpopular because it could promote the acquiring and stockpiling of chemical weapons worldwide. Recently the idea resurfaced, in an altered form, in the U.S.-USSR agreement on destruction of chemical weapons. Both countries may keep 500 tons of chemical agents until sufficient participation is achieved in a multilateral ban. There are several reasons why a minimal stockpile is a good idea:

- A chemical weapons ban cannot be verified effectively;
- Many states may cheat, even if they sign the ban;
- There are indications that some chemical weapons–capable nations will not sign the ban anyway;
- Deterrence has been proven to work;
- Minimal stockpiles would allow for development of international standards for safety and security of chemical weapons stockpiles that are likely to exist.

One could argue that a policy of minimal stockpiles would be as unverifiable as a global ban because nations could have secret stockpiles and covert production capabilities. Nevertheless, a nation is unlikely to attack another with chemical weapons if the other is known to have a chemical weapons stockpile too. This holds true, even if the first nation has more chemical weapons than the one attacked, first because of the threat of counterattack with chemical weapons. Second, with the obvious know-how to make chemical weapons, the attacked nation is likely to produce more chemical weapons quickly, which will provide an extended threat to the initial user. Third, the attacked nation is likely to have some experience or plans relevant to chemical weapons defense and thus will have some chance of repelling initial use.

Essentially, the policy of minimal stockpiles uses the principles evident in World War II and operational in the NATO–Warsaw Pact context since that time: if a nation does not want to be attacked with chemical weapons it should not use them against a nation that possesses them. Limited stockpiles as a deterrent, coupled with a policy of sanctions, are not as noble as a global ban. However, they may bring more stability and reduce the likelihood that chemical weapons would be used. Additionally, the stockpiles that exist could be made safer. Perhaps through an international agreement limiting and making subject to inspection any nation's chemical weapons stockpile. International standards of safety (such as binary weapons and specialized storage) and security (particularly from theft or misuse) could be applied to all stockpiles.

Arguments against the notion of minimal stockpiles are basically political. Such a policy would admit that the global ban is not verifiable and is thus not "good arms control." Furthermore, it would sanction chemical weapons in all states, including states like Iraq and Libya. It does not matter that they have and will continue to have chemical weapons production capability. Even with the destruction of Iraq's chemical plants in the Gulf War, know-how survives and production facilities can be rebuilt.

In conclusion, current policies of export controls and global bans are very unlikely to prevent chemical weapons proliferation and use. Alternatives are complicated and politically unappealing. If current trends continue, there may be a global ban that will basically be a rehash of the Geneva Protocol of 1925—that is, promises by all with no means to enforce them. The difference between the ban and the 1925 protocol is that the United States will forfeit its chemical weapons capability and comply with the provisions of the ban while others probably will not. U.S. troops and civilians might die terrible deaths because a nation using chemical weapons feared no counterattack.

NOTES

1. W. Seth Carus, "Iraq: A Threatening New Superpower," *Moment,* December 1989, p. 52.

2. Deborah Pugh, "Sudan May Have Chemical Arms," *Manchester Guardian,* August 13, 1990, p. 4.

3. Department of Commerce, Bureau of Export Administration, "Report to the Congress on Expansion and Imposition of Foreign Policy Export Controls on Certain Chemicals," December 1989, p. 2. Available from the U.S. Department of Commerce, Office of Public Affairs.

4. David T. Jones, "Eliminating Chemical Weapons: Less Than Meets the Eye," *The Washington Quarterly,* Spring 1989, p. 84.

5. Peter Adams, "Verifying Chemical Weapon Treaty a Delicate Balance," *Defense News,* April 16, 1990, p. 22.

6. "Memorandum of Understanding Between the Government of the United States of America and the Union of Soviet Socialist Republics Regarding a Bilateral Verification Experiment and Data Exchange Related to Prohibition of Chemical Weapons" (Washington D.C.: U.S. Arms Control and Disarmament Agency, September 23, 1989).

7. Andy Pasztor, "Destruction of U.S., Soviet Stockpiles of Chemical Arms Is Many Years Away," *Wall Street Journal,* June 1, 1990, p. 12.

8. UN Security Council, "Report of the Mission Dispatched by the Secretary-General to Investigate Allegations of the Use of Chemical Weapons in the Conflict between the Islamic Republic of Iran and Iraq," S/19823, April 25, 1988, p. 15. Available from the UN Publications Office.

7

Biological and Toxin Agents

Biological warfare agents are living organisms (e.g., bacteria or fungi), viruses, or infective material derived from them that depend for their effects on the ability to multiply in the person, animal, or plant attacked. Biological weapons spread these agents to harm or destroy an enemy. Centuries ago, soldiers threw plague-infested carcasses over the walls of enemy cities to infect the population within. White settlers in America gave blankets infected with smallpox to hostile Indian tribes. And in World War I and World War II there were claims that biological weapons were used. There are also documented cases in which they were used for assassinations.

While most claims have not been proven, it is known that during and since World War II dozens of diseases, primarily those caused by viruses or bacteria, have been studied as possible biological weapons.[1] The Japanese program (1936–45) was extensive, including research on weaponizing the plague, anthrax, cholera, typhoid, and paratyphoid fevers.[2] The Japanese are known to have experimented on prisoners, as did the Germans. Table 3 lists some of the biological agents usable as weapons against people.

Plants and animals also can be targets of biological weapons. The user might want to damage an enemy's food supply or eliminate an economically important product such as an export crop or animal product. Tables 4 and 5 list some of the agents that could be used against nonhuman targets. It should be noted that some animal diseases can also be harmful to humans. Additionally, pathogens harmful only to animals may mutate, creating a variant of the disease that infects humans.

Unlike most other types of weapons, biological weapons can be used

Table 3
Possible Antipersonnel Agents

Disease	Agent	Mortality (percent untreated)	Incubation period (days)	Duration of effects (days)
Anthrax (pulmonary)	Bacillus anthracis	99	1–7	1–7
Bacillary dysentery	Shigella dysenteriae	2–20	1–3	2–10
Botulism	Clostridium botulinum	60–90	.5–3	7–35
Brucellosis	Brucella suis	2–3	14–28	30–120
Cholera	Vibrio comma	10–80	1–7	1–30
Coccidioidomycosis	Coccidioides immitis	unknown (low)	7–14	14–90
Dengue fever	Dengue fever	1–15	5–8	3–35
Diphtheria	Corynebacterium diphtheriae	17–20	1–7	4–14
Eastern equine encephalitis	Eastern equine encephalitis	50–80	4–8	extremely variable
Histoplasmosis	Histoplasma capsulatum	unknown (low)	6–14	months-years
Infectious hepatitis	Infectious hepatitis	0–1	15–40	21–60
Influenza	Influenza	0–1	1–2	7–21
Japanese B encephalitis	Japanese B encephalitis	15–60	7–21	21–90
Plague (pneumonic)	Pasteurella pestis	90–100	2–4	14
"Q" fever	Coxiella burnetti	0–4	14–26	6–10
Rocky Mountain spotted fever	Rickettsia rickettsii	20–80	4–8	14–21
Scrub typhus	Rickettsia tsutsugamushi	1–60	10–12	10–14
Smallpox	Smallpox	5–40	10–16	6–16
Food poisoning	Staphylococcus aureus	0–5	2–3 hours	hours-days
Tuberculosis	Mycobacterium tuberculosis	7–10	21–56	months-years
Tularemia	Pasteurella tularensis	6–8	2–4	14–30

Table 3 (Continued)

Disease	Agent	Mortality (percent untreated)	Incubation period (days)	Duration of effects (days)
Typhoid fever	Salmonella typhosa	5–10	8–14	10–14
Venezuelan equine encephalitis	Venezuelan equine encephalitis	0–1	2–5	3–23
Western equine encephalitis	Western equine encephalitis	7–20	4–8	extremely variable
Yellow fever	Yellow fever	6–60	2–10	10–21

Source: U.S. Dept. of the Army, Biological Laboratory, *Graphic Summary of Selected Infectious Diseases* (Ft. Detrick, Md.: 1960).

either overtly or covertly. In the case of overt use, a military target might be hit with a highly infectious, fast-acting pathogen that would either weaken or kill its victims. Biological weapons would probably be used as a first strike that might go undetected, followed by a conventional attack. Alternatively, biological weapons could be used covertly, with no follow-up attack or other activity that might identify the user. For example, someone could release deadly aerosol agents in a crowded city or dust a virus over crops, using a small private plane. There are many possible scenarios.

Biological weapons have several characteristics that make their covert use feasible. First, the effects of an attack might be considered a natural catastrophe by the victims. A particularly virulent strain of influenza, for example, might be spread purposefully by an enemy and not be perceived as an attack because flu epidemics, although of lesser potency, are not unusual.

Even if a victim suspected a biological weapons attack, it would be hard to prove or to ascertain the identity of the perpetrator. Hypothetically, a government that wanted to conduct genocide against people in a particular region could do so and claim the outbreak was natural. Iraqi Kurds, an ethnic minority, claimed that a typhoid outbreak among their ranks might have been purposefully caused by the Iraqi government.[3]

Another characteristic enabling covert use of biological weapons is that their effects may be slow to develop. For example, an aggressor who wants to inflict unattributable damage could spread diseases to destroy domestic animals such as cattle or sheep, causing a severe blow to the

Table 4
Possible Antianimal Agents

Disease	Agent	Mortality (percent)	Incubation period (days)	Animals affected
African swine fever	African swine fever	95–100	5–9	swine
Anthrax	Bacillus anthracis	40–80	3–7	cattle, goats, sheep
Brucellosis	Brucella suis	Low	30–120	cattle, swine
Foot-and-mouth	Foot-and-mouth	5–50	2–14	cattle, sheep, swine
Fowl plague	Fowl plague	95–100	3–5	chickens
Hog cholera	Hog cholera	80–90	3–7	swine
Newcastle disease	Newcastle disease	5–90	4–8	chickens
Rift Valley fever	Rift Valley fever	10–25	1–3	cattle, sheep
Rinderpest	Rinderpest	15–95	3–9	cattle, goats, sheep, oxen, water buffalo
Venezuelan equine encephalitis	Venezuelan equine encephalitis	60–90	3–10	equines

Source: U.S. Dept. of the Army, Biological Laboratory, *Graphic Summary of Selected Infectious Diseases* (Ft. Detrick, Md.: 1960).

enemy's food supply. The effects on the general population and the economy might not be felt for weeks or months.

The effectiveness of biological weapons is enhanced because the effects of some diseases may not be readily apparent. For example, diseases (especially viruses) that affect plants are potent, but their presence cannot be detected until damage is extensive. They therefore might be used when the objective is to deprive a population of a food source or a crop upon which it is economically dependent (i.e., a staple or a principal food export).

Biological weapons are ideal for covert use, in part because they are

Table 5
Possible Anticrop Agents

Disease	Agent	Crops affected	Reproductive cycle[a] (days)
Black rot	Xanthomanas campestris	cabbage, turnips, broccoli, radish	7–20
Curly top of beets	Curly top	sugar beets, beans, tomatoes	–
Rice blast	Piricularia oryzae	rice	10–18
Rye stem rust	Puccinia graminus secalis	rye	8–12
Smut of corn	Ustilago maydis	corn	7–21
Tobacco mosaic	Tobacco mosaic	tobacco, tomatoes, peppers, turnips	–
Wheat stem rust	Puccinia graminus tritici	wheat	8–12

a. Time organism requires to reproduce itself and be available for natural transmission to other crops.
Source: U.S. Dept. of the Army, Chemical Corps School, *Military Application of Microbiology and Biological Agents,* Special Text 3–162 (Ft. McClellan, Ala.: September 1961).

so easy to deliver. Aerosol cans are simple to produce and can contain a sufficient quantity of the biological agent to cause catastrophe. Alternatively, the agent can simply be placed on the ground. Air currents, vibrations from passing vehicles, or human beings could effectively disseminate the agent. The fact that very small quantities of biological weapons can have devastating effects is shown by the example of tularemia, which is caused by the bacterium *Pasteurella tularensis.* The average size of this bacterium is about 0.2 by 0.5 microns. One cubic inch could contain slightly more than 780,000,000,000,000 of these bacteria; a baseball-sized container (about 12.5 cubic inches) could contain approximately 10,000,000,000,000,000 tuleremia bacteria. If we assume that the contents of the baseball-sized container were disseminated and that 99.9 percent of the bacteria died, that still leaves 10,000,000,000,000 bacteria living. Next assume that five hours after dissemination 99.9 percent of those bacteria die, leaving 10,000,000,000 living. If the number of organisms needed to cause infection is ten, there would be enough bacteria to cause disease in a billion people.[4] Of course, it is impossible to distribute the bacteria evenly, but the example demonstrates that only a small amount is needed to cause disaster.

Although it is difficult to obtain even dispersal, biological weapons can be effective over large areas. This was proven by researchers conducting field tests using harmless bacteria and zinc-cadmium sulphide particles. In one experiment, particles were sprayed from a ship along a 150-mile stretch of U.S. coastline.[5] Particles spread over an estimated 55,000 square miles of land, over which a minimum dose of 15 to a maximum dose of 15,000 particles was inhaled by the affected population.[6] If this had been Q fever, of which a single particle can cause infection, the result could have been that practically everyone in the area would have been infected.[7]

It is also feasible to deliver biological weapons via a water supply. Research has shown that drinking 100 ml of water from a reservoir of some 5 million litres capacity would cause serious infection or intoxication if as little as a half a kilogram of salmonella, 5 kg of botulinum toxin, or 7 kg of staphylococcal enterotoxin had been introduced.[8] To achieve the same effect with chemicals, 10 tons of potassium cyanide would be required.[9] Thus, much smaller quantities of biological weapons would be required to cause the same damage as much larger amounts of chemical weapons.

Who would use such weapons? The United States has renounced biological weapons and does not possess them. There are several less-developed countries known to be engaged in biological weapons research and development. The Soviet Union is also known to be in possession of such weapons. These two groups are discussed in this chapter. Terrorists, another potential user, are not examined; however, it should be emphasized that terrorists could, with dedicated effort, produce and use biological weapons.

Technical Problems with Using Biological Weapons

In recent history, biological weapons agents were not considered feasible tools of modern warfare for a number of reasons. Stability was a primary problem. Bacterial agents, for example, decompose rapidly. Freeze-drying and chemical treatment can lengthen shelf life but only for a matter of weeks. Viral agents are easier to store as they have no metabolic requirements; they do not need to eat or breathe. But because they cannot repair themselves if damaged, they must be handled carefully in the process of dissemination. Sunlight, for example, can harm viruses, making it necessary to use such weapons at night.

Controlling the effects of biological weapons is also considered a major problem. Once disseminated in a population, the speed and extent of their effects are unpredictable. Weather can be an important factor; rain, sunshine, wind, or variable temperatures can all affect the spread of biological weapons. Depending on conditions and on the nature of the agent itself, biological weapons may require days or even weeks to take effect. An aggressor who wants quick action against the enemy would not want to trust the fate of an attack to a force so fickle as the weather. Thus, in the past biological weapons were viewed by military strategists as too difficult to control.

Another drawback of biological weapons agents is that they can remain effective for years, rendering territory unusable and uninhabitable for generations. The use of anthrax on the island of Gruinard off the northwest coast of Scotland provides an example. The island was used from 1941–43 by the British experiments with biological weapons. Anthrax, caused by the bacteria *Bacillus anthracis,* can be contracted by mammals and is highly infectious. Anthrax spores, which can remain dormant but dangerous for years, cause serious, often fatal disease after being inhaled or ingested. Gruinard was plagued by the presence of anthrax spores from 1942 until 1990, when the United Kingdom announced that the island finally had been cleaned.

Another drawback is that biological weapons may accidentally infect the user or the user's plants or animals. Any nation or terrorist that uses biological weapons would want to have an antidote, antibiotics, or a vaccine against the weapon to avoid or counter its effects. Developing such a counter is a much more difficult and expensive task than designing the weapon itself. Developing vaccines is particularly difficult, time-consuming, and costly. Adding to the cost overall is the logistically demanding effort of vaccinating the population. All of this is further complicated by the fact that biological weapons agents may mutate, rendering the therapy or vaccine ineffective.

Effects of Genetic Engineering

Prior to the 1970s, a nation contemplating the use of biological weapons faced serious technical difficulties. Conducting research on the effects of diseases was highly dangerous; mutation of the genes in potential biological weapons agents could not be controlled or "designed"; the agents, once isolated, were often unstable for storage or weapons applications; and some agents were difficult to manufacture in quantity. In particular, viruses required living tissues in which to reproduce, making their manufacture time-consuming and costly.

Genetic engineering and other biotechnology advances have eliminated or reduced most of the problems with researching or manufacturing biological weapons agents. In early 1970, the first successful experiments using DNA recombinant technology were completed. This technology enables researchers to change the genetic material of bacteria, viruses, fungi, and other organisms precisely at will.

Subsequently, scientists discovered an enzyme that allows them to utilize a process called reverse transcription. For example, scientists could identify and transfer toxin-producing genes to other organisms to make more harmful viruses. Harmful genes of the viruses could also be cloned and manufactured very quickly without the traditional dangers to workers. These and many other techniques have allowed scientists to significantly reduce the time, cost, and danger of mass-producing genetically tailored bacteria and viruses.

Genetic engineering can also be used to make viruses more deadly. This is advantageous not only because the disease will spread more rapidly and with greater effect but also because less of the agent is required. The same genetic engineering techniques can be used to develop vaccines.

Biological Weapons: Hard to Develop?

Any country that wants to develop biological weapons can do so with ease, without much risk of detection. Any well-equipped microbiological laboratory with normally skilled technical personnel can produce large quantities of the agents if infectious strains of micro-organisms are available.[10] Also, it is easy to produce micro-organisms covertly. The actual installation need be no bigger than an average size church or small factory.[11] Indeed, most modern hospitals have laboratories capable of isolating strains of diseases usable as biological weapons. However, producing the agents entails all the difficulties mentioned above—safety, instability, and mass production.

Currently, laboratories in many countries around the world have genetic engineering capabilities. The knowledge involved cannot be subject to export controls. Not only is genetic engineering research conducted in many countries by citizens from virtually every country on the globe, but it is also inextricably related to a moral, legitimate application—control and treatment of disease.

Who Has Biological Weapons?

In 1988, CIA Director William Webster said that at least ten nations are developing biological weapons. This number is almost certainly too low. One of those countries is Iraq, which is said to be developing weapons that can spread typhoid, cholera, and anthrax.[12] Until the Gulf War, work was being conducted at a laboratory south of Baghdad near Salman Pak. Iraq had several other facilities where research and manufacturing could have been located. For example, it had a pharmaceutical complex—the Al Kindi Company for Serum and Vaccine Production —built by French contractors. Even though many of these facilities were damaged or destroyed in the war, they will not be very difficult to rebuild. In the future, Iraq will probably place such facilities underground to make sabotage or attack more difficult. Even if it does not try to hide its biological weapons activities, they may be hard to detect. This is because no large-scale research or production facilities are required to produce biological weapons, and there are no distinctive features that would indicate the presence of such a program.

The Soviet biological weapons program is the most closely watched, yet there is little public information on it. The 1989 Pentagon assessment of Soviet military power says only:

> The Soviets continue to improve their ability to use biological agents. New biological technologies, including genetic engineering, are being harnessed to improve the toxicity, stability, and military potential of the Soviet biological warfare stocks. . . . The Soviets continue to deny that they have an offensive biological weapons program, but there has been evidence not only to support the existence of research and development but also weaponized agents. The Sverdlovsk biological agent accident of 1979 that resulted in the release of anthrax from a bacteriological warfare

institute provided such evidence and a strong indication that the Soviets have violated the Biological Weapons Convention of 1972.[13]

That the Soviets had (and may still have) a biological weapons program was given credence by a doctor who reportedly treated victims of the Sverdlovsk accident. In a 1990 article published in the Soviet newspaper *Literaturnaya Gazeta,* a doctor who treated accident victims was quoted. He confirmed that the accident was "waste from a bacteriological weapon."[14]

Toxin Weapons

Toxin weapons are poisonous substances produced by living organisms that are used to cause death or injury in an attack. Toxins such as botulinum, for example, could be used as toxin weapons. This definition of toxin weapons applies whether or not the toxin is produced by an organism or by chemical synthesis. Toxin agents, like the chemical weapons agents of which they are a subset, are inanimate and incapable of multiplying.

Toxin agents are often mistakenly thought of as biological weapons, and definitions of biological weapons occasionally include toxin agents.[15] This stems from the fact that toxins were once considered products only of living organisms. The close relationship of toxin to biological weapons was further engrained by the 1972 Biological Weapons Convention, which outlawed the development, production, and stockpiling of biological and toxin weapons. The apparent reason for inclusion of toxin weapons in the convention was that they required facilities similar to those needed for biological weapons. The United States renounced both simultaneously in 1969.[16] The 1972 convention internationalized the U.S. decision.

Toxin weapons are generally more stable and faster acting than biological weapons and therefore more likely to be effective militarily. Very important is the fact that, unlike biological weapons, there is no danger of the agent spreading, reinfecting, mutating, or lying dormant. The toxin disappears with the victim.

Toxin weapons, like biological weapons, can be used covertly, particularly against a person or a small number of people. There are several cases in which toxins are believed to have been used in assassinations.[17] One well-documented case of toxin weapons use was the 1978 assassination of a Bulgarian exile living in London. The victim was stabbed with the point of an umbrella, which deposited a small (1.53 millimeter) pellet containing 0.2 milligrams of the toxin ricin.[18]

It may be difficult to prove that disease or death caused by a toxin is not attributable to natural causes. However, deaths due to toxins are more likely to raise suspicions than those due to diseases. Toxin deaths are not as common and do not ordinarily occur in large numbers. Because toxin weapons act relatively quickly and because it is unusual for a great number of people to be suddenly poisoned, toxin death is not likely to be thought of as a natural phenomenon. It may be difficult to identify the perpetrator with certainty, however.

Historically, toxin weapons have not been used in warfare, and there are many fewer allegations of their use than of biological weapons use. One reason is that an attack with toxins is likely to be quickly perceived as an attack (unlike the effects of biological weapons, which can be mistaken for a natural phenomenon). Another reason is that prior to the advent of genetic engineering toxins were difficult to mass produce. As Stephen Rose pointed out, "Large numbers of creatures and expensive, laborious processes were needed to yield even small quantities of toxin. For example, using refinement techniques available during the late 1960s, the US Government generated only 11 grams of shellfish toxin from several tons of mussels."[19] At the same time, eight tons of contaminated Alaskan butter clams were needed to make one gram of saxitoxin, and it proved impossible to extract militarily significant quantities of red-tide toxin.

Bacterial toxins were easier to produce in large quantities than other toxins because bacteria themselves are relatively easy to grow. For example, there is little difficulty in the industrial production of the bacterial toxins such as botulinus and those from others of the less exotic sources like ricin.[20] Also, once separated from bacteria, the toxins are relatively easy to handle. They can be stored for long periods in airtight metal containers.

Genetic engineering has made mass production of many toxins easier. The gene responsible for a given toxin is identified, separated, multiplied by cloning, and transferred to other host cells. In other words, with gene-splicing, micro-organisms can now be converted into miniature poison factories, permitting the production of militarily significant amounts of toxins at far less cost and effort.[21]

Although the exact cost of producing toxins with genetic engineering procedures cannot be determined, estimates can be made using figures for pharmaceutical production. From research and development to full production can cost thirty to sixty million dollars.[22]

Who Has Toxin Weapons?

One of the countries suspected of working on toxin weapons is Iran. Twice in mid-1989, Iran reportedly attempted to import toxin-producing strains of fungus from Canada and the Netherlands.[23] In December 1988 and again in February 1989, an Iranian representative sought to buy several types of fungus found on grass and wheat that produce mycotoxins.

Some highly trained U.S. biologists scoff at such reports, however. They say there is no need for Iran to buy such materials. They point out that very large numbers of Iranian students have received advanced degrees in the United States and, in the process, have become fully capable of isolating such toxin-producing strains or other materials usable for biological and toxin weapons. For the right price, such experts might be enticed to work in Iran.

Iran might desire toxin weapons if it believes that Iraq has them. In 1984, Iran accused Iraq of using toxins against Iranian troops. Stories in the West German press reported that Iraq had bought small quantities of toxins from a West German company.

In conclusion, biological and toxin weapons can be produced by university-level biologists in hospital and university facilities available in many countries. The better the facilities and training, the better the capabilities. This is particularly true insofar as genetic engineering is concerned. Detecting such activities will be nearly impossible because of the simple requirements and lack of distinguishing features of such activity. The only way that such work might be exposed would be through the revelations of those directly involved in the research.

NOTES

1. Erhard Geissler, "A New Generation of Biological Weapons," in *Biological and Toxin Weapons Today* (New York: Oxford University Press, 1986), pp. 22, 23.

2. John Cookson and Judith Nottingham, *A Survey of Chemical and Biological Warfare* (New York: Monthly Review Press, 1969), p. 296.

3. Stephen Engelberg, "Iraq Said to Study Biological Arms," *New York Times,* January 18, 1989, p. A7.

4. This example was provided by Brig. Gen. David A. Nydam, commander of the U.S. Army Chemical Research, Development, and Engineering Center.

5. One bacteria used in the experiment off the coast of San Francisco was *Serratia marcesceus,* which was thought to be harmless in 1950 when field tests were conducted. See "Biological Warfare Trials at San Francisco, California, 20–27 September 1950," U.S. Chemical Corps Biological Laboratories, Special Report 142, January 22, 1951. In 1969, however, the bacteria was recognized to have limited pathogenic capability and precluded for experimental use "because of the assumed role as an opportunist, producing disease if man is exposed to large doses and/or when the body defenses are weakened." From Leonard A. Cole, *Clouds of Secrecy,* (Totowa, N.J.: Rowman & Littlefield, 1988), pp. 167–68.

6. I. Malek, "Biological Weapons," in *CBW: Chemical and Biological Warfare,* ed. Steven Rose (Boston: Beacon Press, 1969), p. 51.

7. Cookson and Nottingham, *A Survey of Chemical and Biological Warfare,* p. 267.

8. Malek, "Biological Weapons," p. 52.

9. Cookson and Nottingham, *A Survey of Chemical and Biological Warfare,* p. 269.

10. Malek, "Biological Weapons," p. 52.

11. Cookson and Nottingham, *A Survey of Chemical and Biological Warfare,* p. 264.

12. Engelberg, "Iraq Said to Study Biological Arms."

13. U.S. Department of Defense, *Soviet Military Power: Prospects for Change, 1989,* p. 68. Available from the U.S. Department of Defense, Office of Public Affairs.

14. Natalya Zenova, "Military Secret: Reasons for the Tragedy in Sverdlovsk Must be Investigated," *Literaturnaya Gazeta,* August 22, 1990, as reprinted in *Wall Street Journal,* November 28, 1990.

15. Geissler, "A New Generation of Biological Weapons," p. 5.

16. Ibid., p. 18.

17. Neil C. Livingstone and Joseph D. Douglass, Jr., *CBW: The Poor Man's Atom Bomb* (Cambridge, Mass.: Institute for Foreign Policy Analysis, February 1984), p. 17. Instances when biological weapons are thought to have been used for assassination are in Robert Harris and Jeremy Paxman, *A Higher Form of Killing* (New York: Hill and Wang, 1982).

18. "Clues to the Pinhead Poison That Killed Georgi Markov," *Manchester Guardian Weekly,* November 8, 1981, p. 8.

19. Stephen Rose, "The Coming Explosion of Silent Weapons," *Naval War College Review,* Summer 1989, p. 13.

20. Cookson and Nottingham, *A Survey of Chemical and Biological Warfare,* p. 265.

21. Stephen Rose, "The Coming Explosion of Silent Weapons," p. 13.

22. Sharon Gebley and Nadine Joseph, "The Pharmacy of the Seas," *Newsweek,* May 21, 1990, p. 78.

23. Michael R. Gordon and Stephen Engelberg, "Iran Is Said to Try to Obtain Toxins," *New York Times,* August 13, 1989, p. 11.

8
Ballistic and Cruise Missiles: Hard to Develop?

Countries seeking ballistic missiles have experienced increasing difficulty obtaining them in the marketplace because of the extensive export controls enacted by most supplier countries. To avoid controls, restrictive conditions, or the possibility of a supply cutoff, nations often try to develop ballistic missiles indigenously. Though the objective is to avoid reliance on foreign technology, importing some equipment greatly shortens the process of missile development. For this reason, some nations disguise their objective and instead claim that their goal is to develop a satellite launch vehicle (SLV).

SLVs versus Ballistic Missiles

Ballistic missiles are launched with rocket motors to a certain altitude and then use gravity to coast to earth. Their initial trajectory is determined by an inertial guidance system that typically drops off with the missile booster stage at burnout, anywhere from one to six minutes after launch. The missiles continue on their trajectory essentially unguided and incapable of being corrected should they deviate from the intended flight path.

SLVs are also launched with rocket motors and use inertial guidance. Because they are intended to deliver satellites into orbit, SLVs are large and powerful. Their characteristics are similar to intercontinental ballistic missiles. The technologies used to launch and guide SLVs are virtually indistinguishable from those of ballistic missiles.

Because of the similar technologies, a country can pursue ballistic missiles while pretending to be working on SLVs, making foreign technical assistance more obtainable. Also, feigning an interest in SLVs might lessen the chance that neighboring countries will be upset and inspired to build their own missiles. Even if a nation has no intention of developing weapons when it begins an SLV program, the technology can later be applied to ballistic missiles.

The interchangeability of SLV and ballistic missile technology has been demonstrated on several occasions. In 1987, the United States refurbished versions of its vintage 1961 Atlas intercontinental ballistic missile (ICBM) to use as an SLV. Also, a Titan II ICBM was used to launch Gemini capsules in the 1960s. The Soviet Union is considering a venture to market its SS-20 ballistic missiles as SLVs. Most present-day U.S. and Soviet SLVs are descendants of ballistic missiles.

To develop either an SLV or a ballistic missile, a nation must gain expertise in four areas: propellants, missile design, guidance and control, and support functions. Additionally, it must have the technical infrastructure necessary to manufacture and test the components as designed. Although missile research, development, and manufacture present a variety of tough technical challenges to a country, the greatest obstacles are usually the development of guidance and control systems and propellant technologies.

Solid Propellants

There are two types of propellants used in rockets: solid and liquid. Each presents very different problems in missile design and manufacture. About 90 percent of all solid propellants in use today are a composite which contains an oxidizer (usually 60 to 70 percent by total weight), a metal fuel (15 to 20 percent, usually aluminum), organic binder (5 to 10 percent), and a number of minor additives. One of the most popular solid propellant oxidizers, ammonium perchlorate, provides a good example of the types of problems and level of difficulty involved in propellant manufacture.

The major commercial-scale use for ammonium perchlorate (AP) is as the main element of solid propellant for missiles. Although more expensive to produce than alternatives such as ammonium nitrate, AP usually performs better and operates well despite extreme changes in temperature. Also, because it is very dense, AP allows for smaller rocket motor design.

AP is an inorganic chemical that looks like sugar. It was developed and first used in the mining industry in the 1800s. The basic chemistry is well documented. Thus, it is not difficult for a country to obtain information on exactly how to make AP and how to use it.

Manufacturing AP is not very complex, but it is also not easy. Certain problems must be avoided. In particular, for use in propellants, the AP must be almost 100 percent pure. AP can easily be contaminated with impurities such as iron or nickel by the vessels in which it is processed.

When AP is combined with other raw materials to make propellant, it must be free of moisture. This is why feeding, mixing, and casting of AP propellant is usually done in arid areas. Moisture-contaminated AP can degrade propellant performance and rocket motor reliability.

Another difficulty is that AP can explode when heated or impacted. Two conditions enhance the risk: smaller crystals and greater impurities. To limit the hazard of explosion during shipment, AP is usually shipped as large particles and then reduced in size, if needed, by the propellant manufacturer.

The equipment used to make AP is not unique. Tanks, pipes, pumps, and other items used in chemical plants are necessary. Because of the corrosive nature of some of the chlorine salts involved, certain pumps and heat exchangers must be made of special materials such as titanium. Also, polyethylene liners are required for some of the vessels. Equipment of this nature is used for a variety of chemical-industrial processes and is commercially available. The materials used to make AP are also common: table salt and other simple, easily obtainable chemicals such as ammonium chlorate, a bleach used in the paper industry.

The key to making AP or any other solid propellant ingredient is experience. While equipment and formulas are readily available, the know-how to safely produce chemical compounds is as much an art as it is a science. Giving a person eggs, flour, butter, and a recipe does not guarantee that he or she will repeatedly produce quality pastries. With an experienced chef, such a guarantee is credible. Similarly, any country that has a well-developed chemical industry could produce solid propellants. While care must be taken, it is no more complex or demanding than other processes dealing with corrosive chemicals. A country without such experience is likely to have difficulty fulfilling the numerous requirements for safety and purity.

While the chemical manufacturing aspects of producing solid propellants are not difficult to overcome for the more industrialized countries, shaping the propellant can be a daunting task. Solid propellant is generally shaped in a cylinder with a star-shaped mandrel running along its length. (The propellant burns outward from the cavity.) After the propellant is cured, the mandrel is removed in a hazardous operation that is conducted remotely. Casting or pressing the propellant is very hazardous and complex. Friction must be avoided. Also, the bonding between the walls of the rocket case and the propellant must be secure. If the propellant were to separate from the walls, burning would be uneven, perhaps causing explosion or loss of control.

Liquid Propellants

With solid-propellant rockets, the challenge is in making the propellant. With liquid-propellant rockets, the greatest difficulty is in making the motor.

Liquid propellant production is relatively easy for any country capable of refining petroleum, producing fertilizer, manufacturing dyes, etc. The chemicals used in liquid propellants are quite common. Liquid oxygen, hydrogen peroxide, and nitric acid are three oxidizers that serve a host of chemical-industrial functions and are widely available. Kerosene, aniline, hydrazine, and ethyl alcohol are fuels that are readily acquired. Such chemicals, because they have so many applications, are produced by many companies in many countries.

Manufacturing chemicals for liquid propellants involves processes that are well known and well documented. As with solid propellants, purity is necessary for safety and performance reasons. The primary problems facing a country that does not produce the chemicals used in liquid propellants would be the cost of constructing a single-purpose chemical plant and instituting rigorous safety requirements.

Safety is also a primary concern in storage and transportation of liquid propellants. Although standard means such as drums, rail tank cars, and tank trucks can be used, handling must entail procedures to prevent spills or contamination. Those propellants that are corrosive require special equipment such as stainless steel containers or piping, inert plastics for seals or gaskets, and special lubricants for bearings or valve stems.

The fact that some liquid rocket propellants are highly toxic and must be handled and stored with great care was amply demonstrated by a May 1990 tragedy in the Soviet Union. Rocket fuel leaked from a storage tank at the Soviet submarine base at Severodvinsk on the White Sea.[1] Over 100,000 seals and millions of other marine animals died. Soviet officials reported that at least one-third of all marine life in the White Sea perished. The animals that survived are likely to be seriously damaged by the toxicity of the fuel. Soviet officials ordered that no fish from the sea are to be sold or eaten.

Cryogenic liquid propellants are much more difficult to handle. Hydrogen, for example, is highly combustible across a range of temperatures and quantities. Moreover, a hydrogen flame is invisible to the naked eye. To ensure safety, instruments capable of detecting the accumulation of hydrogen and hydrogen-oxygen flames must be used and monitored continually.

Cryogenic propellants are liquified gases at low temperatures; they evaporate rapidly at ambient temperatures. When used in a missile, the supply must be replenished regularly to make up for evaporation losses. In manufacture and transport, special insulated tanks, pipes, and valves are needed. These items, while specialized, are not unusual in the chemical industry and are available on the open market.

Table 6
Comparative Advantages of Propellant Types

Liquids	Solids
On-site fueling necessary for most liquid propellants	Ready to fire
Complex engineering	Relatively simple engineering
Easier chemistry	Difficult chemistry and casting/pressing
Higher specific impulse: more thrust per unit of weight	More thrust per unit of volume (more compact)

Liquid Rocket Motors

Rocket motors present difficult design challenges because they are essentially controlled explosions. Temperatures inside the rocket motor may be more than 5,000° F as the fuel burns.

Liquid rocket motors have a host of complex components such as injector nozzles (which regulate a fine spray of propellant for mixture in the combustion chamber), valves, pipes, chambers, flow control devices, igniters, pumps, and moving parts. Designing these to operate under high temperature, severe vibration, and other stresses is very difficult.

Designing liquid-propellant rocket motors is complicated because materials that can withstand heat and other stresses must be used but must be cooled to a temperature below that of the combustion chamber. To accomplish this, it is necessary to design a series of coils, pumps, and valves to assure that the fuel flows evenly around the outside of the motor. An engineering or construction flaw could lead to clogged valves or other fuel flow problems, causing the motor to explode.

If a nation succeeds in designing a workable liquid-propellant rocket motor there is still the obstacle of manufacturing it. High standards must be kept to assure that a number of the motors can be built and that all or most of them will perform as expected.

Although rocket motor design is technically challenging, a number of factors make it easier today than it was a decade or two ago. The amount of data and technology available from open sources—universities, literature, computer databases—make the design task much easier. Many foreign rocket designers learned the basics by working in the rocket programs of industrialized countries. They have gained additional information by examining missiles purchased abroad. Despite this information and training, rocket design and construction is difficult. Producing large numbers of missiles for weapons use requires consistent quality control to ensure that an adequate number work properly.

Guidance

While designing rockets today is easier, guidance systems are still difficult for less-developed countries to master. To be accurate, a missile must "know" its velocity and orientation. A ballistic missile must be placed very precisely at a given point in space, angled exactly so as to enter a specific orbit, and travel at a precise velocity. A tiny error in any of these variables can result in significant degradation of accuracy.

The American MX ballistic missile, for example, has a range of 10,000 kilometers or more and is injected into its orbit at an angle of 27° from the local horizon. Because the final velocity of the MX is nearly 23,000 feet per second at burnout (when the missile is injected into its orbit), it has to be accurate to less than 1 foot per second. If the velocity of the MX is off by 1 foot per second, an error of .9 nautical miles in range results.

To be practical, missiles must be deliverable to different targets at varying ranges. This requires that the missile be able to change its velocity or injection angle. To sense the velocity of the missile at the time propulsion is cut off, accelerometers are used. To sense the angular orientation of the missile, gyroscopes are used. These two instruments comprise the missile's inertial navigation unit and are the two most difficult guidance components for a less-developed country to design and manufacture.

Countries often encounter errors in design and implementation of accelerometers and gyroscopes. Design errors occur when the engineering tools are not up to the task of construction. They include bad bearings, temperature-sensitive electronics, slow clock rates, or bad software in the guidance computer. Implementation errors arise when some aspect of the construction results in poor performance. For example, even if the gyroscope performs perfectly when independent of the missile, its use with the missile may create problems.

The gyroscope, which points the missile toward a precise position in space at burnout in order for it to hit its target, must be highly accurate. For example, a 1 milliradian (1/20 of one degree) error in the alignment of the axis can result in the missile landing one or more nautical miles off target.

The need for accuracy is one factor that makes the gyroscopes used in aircraft inappropriate for use in missiles. If a country were to buy a gyroscope intended for aircraft and place it in a missile, the missile would be very inaccurate—probably by several miles. To have an effect on the intended target, the country might try to fit the missile with a nuclear, chemical, or biological warhead.

In summary, solid propellants are more difficult to make than liquid. Liquid-propellant motors, however, provide a very serious technical challenge. In the case of either type of missile, the guidance system presents difficulties to a proliferator. Guidance for missiles is feasible with commercially available equipment used in aircraft, but it presents many technical problems and would probably still result in significant errors.

Cruise Missiles

To date, cruise missiles have not been a factor in proliferation. Most countries attempting to develop delivery systems have focused on ballistic missiles. (The reasons for this are discussed in the following chapter.) The potential for a shift toward development of cruise missiles by many nations is great, however.

One reason that cruise missiles are likely to become a proliferation problem is that the technology is relatively simple and readily available. Small aircraft, particularly those with jet engines, make more than adequate cruise missiles. Adapting an aircraft navigation system to make a cruise missile is a much simpler task than converting it for ballistic missile guidance. A nation need not develop highly sophisticated, ground-hugging cruise missiles to be effective. Being on-target is the important factor.

In 1992, guidance for cruise missiles will become even simpler. That year, the global positioning system (GPS) will be fully operational. GPS is a series of satellite markers (fourteen are aloft as of mid-1990; all of the twenty-four planned markers are to be orbiting by the end of 1992) that emit signals for navigation. The system can be used by anyone with a GPS receiver, a small device that "reads" a signal and calculates exact location. One GPS broadcast is open and gives a reading accurate to within 100 meters. A second broadcast is ordinarily encrypted. Any country can use the open broadcast GPS by buying a lower-performance GPS receiver. Some seven thousand are already in use by civilians in the United States.[2] Military receivers capable of decoding the highly accurate broadcast are not publicly available and cost about $40,000 each.[3] Less-capable, available receivers cost as little as $3,000.[4] Any country could purchase a GPS receiver on the open market and use it to guide cruise missiles to targets with an accuracy of 100 meters or less.

Though GPS was not intended for such use, it could certainly be used in this way. It is also technically possible to shut off the GPS, but the system is increasingly crucial to the safe transit of thousands of commercial aircraft, trains, and ships every day. In the future, incapacitating this system will be increasingly difficult because many lives could be lost in a collapse of transportation dependent on GPS. Any decision to do so would have to be based on proof that the GPS was about to be used for missile delivery.

In summary, ballistic missiles can be developed using the "cover" of satellite launch vehicles; cruise missiles can be built using the cover of aircraft development. Technical obstacles have been difficult but can be overcome with dedicated effort; they are not beyond the capabilities of many developing countries. Guidance has been and probably will continue to be the most difficult obstacle, particularly for ballistic missiles. Cruise missiles may become a greater proliferation problem, in part because the Global Positioning System could be used for guidance, with accuracy to within 100 meters.

NOTES

1. Martin Sieff, "Soviet Officials Admit to 'Ecological Tragedy,' " *Washington Times,* June 29, 1990, p. 8.

2. Vincent Kiernan, "Air Force Alters GPS Signals to Aid Troops," *Space News,* September 24–30, 1990, p. 3.

3. Bob Brewin, "DOD Buys GPS Receivers for Desert Shield," *Federal Computer Week,* September 17, 1990, p. 7.

4. Stan Simon, "New Satellite Navigation System is Called Far Superior to LORAN," *Boston Globe,* December 31, 1990, p. 35.

9
Missile Proliferation: Who and Why?

Without delivery capability, nuclear, chemical, and biological warheads are useless. A terrorist hypothetically could deliver a warhead by land. A chemical or biological weapons canister could, for example, be opened in a crowded city with a timer. Nations at war, however, would have to deliver many such canisters in a fashion that would not endanger their own troops.

In the past, manned aircraft were assumed the most likely way to deliver weapons of mass destruction. Aircraft delivery makes it possible to place a warhead well within an enemy's territory, and certain techniques enable pilots to do so without killing themselves. Aircraft can make on-the-spot corrections for aiming errors, and they are, of course, reusable. Thus, they are cost efficient.

Despite the advantages of air craft, there are at least three reasons why they are no longer considered the optimal means of warhead delivery. First, there has been an increase in air defense capabilities, particularly in regions where weapons of mass destruction are most likely to be used. In the Middle East, which provides the best example, Israeli air defenses are among the best in the world. Dropping a chemical, biological, or nuclear warhead on Israel by airplane would be extremely difficult.

A second disadvantage of airplane delivery is that of range limitation. Many targets may be well out of range for most countries' capabilities. In-flight refueling technology is difficult to acquire because of controls by the United States and other suppliers. Additionally, long flights can be highly taxing on even the most skilled, disciplined pilots. Iraq learned in its war with Iran that ballistic missiles were extremely useful for attacking the enemy well behind the lines. Iraq used upgraded Scud missiles to terrorize Tehran. Had the war gone on, Iraq might have used ballistic missiles to deliver chemical warheads.

Finally, pilot fear and error become factors in airplane warhead delivery. As Iraq discovered in its war with Iran, chemical weapons can be delivered too close to the lines; a wind change can turn an army's own weapon against itself. Use of ballistic missiles releases pilots, who may be frightened or insufficiently trained, from the job of delivery and puts it in the hands of skilled missile operators in well-protected areas.

The main advantages that ballistic missiles present over delivery via manned aircraft are speed and certainty. Missiles travel several times faster than airplanes, are not subject to human fears and errors, and avoid interdiction by most defenses. The proven exception is ballistic missile defense systems such as the Patriot, successfully employed for the first time in January 1991 against Iraqi Scuds in the Gulf War.

There is also the prestige of ballistic missiles. Increasingly, countries have viewed ballistic missile possession as a mark of technological prowess and status.

Another factor behind some nations' drive to acquire missile technology is the desire to launch a satellite. For some of these nations, the prestige of lofting a satellite and the need to put up communications satellites may be motives. Many, however, eventually want to be able to deploy spy satellites.

The fact that many countries are trying to acquire ballistic missiles—and that most of these countries are suspected of developing warheads of mass destruction—makes the whole proliferation problem much more dangerous and urgent. Even in cases where countries obtain missiles but have only conventional warheads—as in the instance of Saudi Arabia's purchase of Chinese CSS-2 missiles—such transfers are dangerous and destabilizing for a number of reasons.

First, there is no guarantee that the missile will not be sold or given to another country, especially one that has warheads of mass destruction. Second, there is no way to preclude the missile being reverse-engineered, built, and sold. This is what happened with the Soviet Scud, which has been independently built and sold by North Korea. Third, neighbors and foes are stimulated to acquire missiles as well, for reasons of defense or prestige. Fourth, intentions can change and often do. A missile purchased for use with a conventional warhead may later be used for delivery of a chemical, biological, or nuclear weapon.

Given that ballistic missiles have such an escalatory effect on the threat posed by proliferation, the extent to which missile capabilities have spread is a crucial component of the overall proliferation problem. At least twenty-two third-world countries already have or are trying to obtain ballistic missiles.[1]

For the most part, nations are seeking intermediate or long-range missile capability. Short-range systems are fairly readily available and much easier to develop indigenously. However, they are not useful as strategic weapons and cannot be used to launch satellites—the two primary goals of many nations. Intermediate-range missiles are harder to develop, particularly if they are intended to be accurate and/or carry a heavy payload. For purposes of this discussion, intermediate-range ballistic missiles are defined as in the Intermediate Nuclear Forces Treaty between the United States and the Soviet Union—ground-launched missiles tested at a range of 500–5,500 kilometers. Ballistic missiles with lesser capability are referred to as short-range missiles. Table 7 lists third-world countries that have or may soon have intermediate-range ballistic missiles.

U.S. and Soviet Missiles

The U.S. and Soviet short-range missiles have had the greatest influence on missile proliferation.[2] The Scud, a Soviet missile with a three-hundred-kilometer range, has probably been most influential. It is a road-transportable, single-stage missile that uses liquid propellant and is fairly simple to manufacture and use. First used in 1965, its modified version was exported beginning in 1973. Egypt, Syria, Libya, North Korea, Iraq, and South Yemen received Scud missiles directly from the Soviets. Some countries subsequently retransferred the missiles, which are now used by at least fifteen countries. The missiles have been manufactured as well in Egypt, Iraq, and North Korea.

Although the Soviet-exported Scud is not an intermediate-range missile (i.e., it has a range of less than 500 kilometers), it has had a direct impact on their proliferation. North Korea successfully upgraded the Scud to exceed a range of 500 kilometers,[3] as did Iraq. Perhaps other countries have or will as well.

The U.S. Lance missile, with a range of 130 kilometers, uses a liquid propellant system. Although the Lance was exported primarily to Western countries that are not known to be developing ballistic missiles, it was

Table 7
Intermediate-Range Ballistic Missiles (IRBM) in the Third World

	System	Range (km)	Payload (kg)	Status
Afghanistan	Scud[1]	300	1,000	imported
Argentina	Condor II[2]	750–1,000	500+	R&D
Brazil	MB/EE 600	500	?	R&D
Egypt	Scud	300	1,000	imported
	Condor II	750–1,000	500+	R&D
India	Agni	600+	1,000+	tested
Iran	Scud	300	1,000	imported
	IRBM	?	?	R&D
Iraq	Scud	500+	500	imported
	Condor II	750–1,000	500+	R&D
Israel	Jericho 2	800+	?	tested
Libya	Scud	300	1,000	imported
North Korea	Scud	300	1,000	reverse-engineered
Pakistan	IRBM	?	?	R&D
Saudi Arabia	CSS2	2,000+	2,000	imported
South Africa	IRBM	500+	?	tested
South Korea	IRBM	?	?	R&D
South Yemen	Scud	300	1,000	imported
Syria	Scud	300	1,000	imported
	IRBM	?	?	R&D
Taiwan	IRBM	?	?	R&D
Vietnam	Scud	300	1,000	imported

1. Although the Scud is usually rated at 300 km, it can readily be upgraded to the intermediate range of 500. Intermediate-range Scuds were used, for example, by Iraq during its war with Iran and in the Gulf War.
2. The Condor is a cooperative program involving Argentina, Egypt, and Iraq that has been put on hold, largely due to financial problems and political pressures by the United States and others.

also sent to Israel and South Korea. The missile programs of both these countries have benefited from Lance technology.

The export of nonballistic missiles, such as surface-to-air (SAM) missiles, has also helped proliferant countries develop their own missile capabilities. South Korea, for example, gained significant experience in missile design and construction when it successfully copied the U.S. Nike Hercules SAM.

Although the implications are not yet clear, the Soviet Union transferred SS-23 missiles—banned from Soviet stockpiles by the INF Treaty—to Eastern European countries, which may influence those countries to develop their own intermediate-range missiles. The Soviets secretly delivered the missiles to East Germany, Czechoslovakia, and Bulgaria.

China

Another major missile supplier, China, is likely to contribute more to proliferation in the future than it has as of early 1990. China has earned hard currency and perhaps political influence from military exports, including the sale of Silkworm missiles to Iran and CSS-2 intermediate-range ballistic missiles to Saudi Arabia. There are a number of other transactions China is suspected of having made, some involving the sale not of missiles but of the technology to make them.

In terms of sales, China's M-series missiles present the greatest worry. China has offered to sell the M-9, with a range of 650 kilometers, to a variety of countries in Latin America and the Middle East. Although there is no evidence that China has actually sold the M-9, there are reports that it has exported other missiles of lesser range from the M-family.[4]

In late 1988, China committed itself to a policy of restraint in the export of missiles. Following talks with the Chinese, U.S. officials made public the fact that, although China would not become party to any Western export control regime, it had agreed not to export intermediate-range missiles. China almost certainly was showing its willingness to respect the "international norm" of the INF Treaty.

Following the Tiananmen Square massacre in 1989, arms control bilaterals between the United States and China were not held as they had been the previous three years. Nevertheless, the United States sought government-to-government dialogue on the issue of missile exports. In December 1989, U.S. national security advisor Brent Scowcroft visited Beijing and asked for assurances. China restated that it would not sell intermediate-range missiles to countries in regions of tension, like the Middle East.[5]

In February 1990, the United States again pressured China on the question of missile sales. China declined to go beyond its previously stated position.[6] While it is very unlikely that China will sell INF-range missiles, it is possible that missiles just under the 500-kilometer range will be sold. Such missiles could be upgraded to have a greater range. It is also possible that China will begin to sell components and/or technology rather than complete missiles.

China's interest in missile (and perhaps satellite) technology transfer may not be purely economic and political but may also be motivated by a desire for access to outside technology. Reportedly a China-Israel-South Africa triangle exists that may involve Israel supplying China with radar technology derived from its Lavi fighter project with the United States.[7] Although Israel and China have been sharing technology since the early 1980s, the exchange has intensified recently. In February 1990, Israel opened an Academy of Sciences in Beijing.[8] Israel is providing China with electronics and guidance systems to modernize its jet aircraft and missiles.

Iraq

Iraq is one of the most dangerous countries in possession of ballistic missiles. It has pursued nuclear weapons capability, has proven its ability to produce and use chemical weapons, and is working on biological weaponry as well. Iraq's conflict with Iran, its hostility toward other Arab states such as Syria, its civil war with the Kurdish minority, and its antipathy toward Israel make it highly likely that Iraq will continue to engage in war. Even if its army is defeated and its infrastructure shattered, Iraq will be dangerous until its leadership changes. Even with a more peaceful government, as in the example of Egypt under Hosni Mubarak, there are likely to be simmering hostilities that can flare up and stimulate Iraqi military development.

Iraq's use of upgraded Scud missiles in the Iran-Iraq war and later in the Gulf War demonstrated that it has intermediate-range ballistic missiles. At the time the Scuds were used against Tehran, it was generally believed that Iraq received outside assistance in upgrading their range from 300 kilometers. Although there is no clear evidence that

Iraq received outside help on the Scuds, it is said to have received missile-related help from European countries. For example, Iraq's Sa'ad 16 Research Center reportedly bought a supersonic wind tunnel designed by an Austrian company and built by West Germany's Aviatest.[9] Computers to support wind tunnel testing were reportedly obtained from the United States.[10] Also, there is a history of underestimating Iraq's capabilities.

Many interested observers, including U.S. the intelligence community, were taken by surprise when Iraq tested a three-stage satellite launch vehicle (SLV) on December 5, 1989. Iraq claimed to have produced the SLV indigenously.[11] It is conceivable that several Scud rocket motors were strapped together to provide enough thrust for the test. U.S. Secretary of Defense Dick Cheney commented: "The booster looked as if it was made up of five short-range rockets. Together the rockets could give the booster a range of about 1,000 kilometers."[12] On December 2, 1990, Iraq again surprised the U.S. military and others by test-firing three intermediate-range ballistic missiles to a distance of over 670 kilometers.[13] Iraq applied its capabilities in the Persian Gulf conflict; it hit Tel Aviv, for example, with a Scud upgraded to intermediate range.

The world learned of Iraq's SLV when the Iraqi government showed the test-firing on television. Without such public displays it is difficult to know the status of Iraq's capabilities, and in the future it could be even more difficult to get information. Iraq established a missile test facility in the west African country of Mauritania,[14] where close observation and interception of telemetry of missile tests will be much more problematical.

Although it is unclear how and where Iraq got its SLV capability, it is known that the Iraqis have been working very hard to develop ballistic missiles for some time. Iraq has sought help from abroad in its efforts, particularly in cooperation with other less developed countries. For example, Iraq has worked extensively with Brazil. Over three hundred Brazilians, including twenty-one "weapons specialists," were stranded in Iraq at the beginning of the 1990 economic embargo.[15] The weapons specialists reportedly had worked on the defunct Brazilian Air Force Piranha missile program, abandoned in 1988 due to high costs. Iraq has also been involved in other multinational efforts with developing countries. It was an active participant in the Condor II effort, the cooperative venture with Argentina and Egypt that began in the early 1980s.

Argentina and the Condor Project

The original Condor ballistic missile project reportedly began in Argentina under the direction of a German manager, with support from as many as one hundred fifty people from Germany, France, and Italy.[16] Messerschmidt-Boelkow-Blohm (MBB), West Germany's largest aerospace group, worked on Condor I. MBB is a partner in the European airbus, is a major contractor for NATO, and specializes in making missiles.[17]

In 1985, Argentina's Condor I was displayed at the Paris air show. It is a solid-propellant rocket that can carry a 400-kilogram payload to an altitude of about 70 kilometers or a range of approximately 100 kilometers.[18] This prototype became the basis for the Condor II ballistic missile, a two-stage rocket to be powered by solid-propellant motors. It is to be capable of carrying a 500 kilogram or greater warhead to a distance of up to 1,000 kilometers.

MBB claimed to withdraw from the Condor project in 1985 due to concerns about the military nature of the project. However, various reports indicate that MBB scientists and engineers continue to work on Condor, perhaps without corporate permission.

When Argentina's missile program suffered from financial problems in 1984, it sought and obtained two Middle Eastern partners in the project. In return, both Egypt and Iraq have the right to produce the Condor II themselves. Because Condor II is expected to be accurate only to 750 meters, it probably would require a chemical, nuclear, or biological warhead to be truly effective.

A crucial characteristic of the Condor program is that it has involved extensive technology transfers from several European companies. In addition to MBB, a Switzerland-based consortium of sixteen companies called Consen S.A. reportedly obtained technology for the Condor project from, among others, the German conglomerate Bolen Industries.[19] By utilizing multiple companies, subsidiaries, and a tangled web of connections, European companies have circumvented export controls. Similarly, subterfuge has been used to obtain missile components from the United States and elsewhere.

The technical and economic problems encountered by the Condor program caused Argentina to reconsider its continuation. In April 1990, Argentina announced that it was halting construction of the Condor. It is not clear whether this is a cessation of the entire project, of the trilateral relationship between Argentina and its Arab partners, or a temporary pause in the program.

Even if the Condor project has been shelved, Argentina is probably continuing research and development that ultimately will enable it to build an intermediate-range ballistic missile like the Condor. The Alacram missile program, for example, was still active in 1990.[20] It is short-range (200 kilometer) but has a payload similar to that of the Condor. Its successful development would be an important step in a missile development program.

Egypt

In addition to its participation in the Condor program, Egypt has made independent efforts to develop ballistic missiles. Although there is not much public data on the effort, some information has surfaced when Egypt has been caught attempting to import illegally certain missile components and technology. In 1988, there was an attempt to smuggle 420 pounds of carbon phenolic cloth—a material used in missiles and stealth aircraft to evade radar and protect parts from intense heat—out of the United States.[21] This case provided some of the best evidence yet of the Egyptian efforts to develop ballistic missiles.

The conspiracy to acquire carbon cloth was financed by Iraq.[22] With the help of Consen S.A., an Egyptian scientist living in California named Abdelkader Helmy, an Egyptian colonel, and others tried to export the material illegally. Although this effort was discovered and thwarted, other such schemes may have succeeded.

When Helmy was tried on smuggling charges, repeated claims were made that the plan was under the direction of Egypt's defense minister, Abdel Halim Abu Ghazala. In April 1989, President Hosni Mubarak removed Abu Ghazala from his position, probably as a direct result of the Helmy affair.[23] Because Abu Ghazala oversaw Egypt's missile development, his removal may have been a setback for Egypt's missile efforts. However, it is clear that Egypt continues its objectives and is likely to seek outside help to achieve them.

One possible source of technical assistance is China. Reportedly, China has agreed to help Egypt modernize its production of surface-to-air and surface-to-surface missiles under a protocol signed between the two countries in June 1990.[24] The agreement apparently entails enabling Egypt's missile factory to produce newer versions of the Scud.

Egyptian officials remain highly motivated to either have Israel reduce its ballistic missile capabilities or to increase their own. They believe that Israel is receiving significant technical help in missile development through the Arrow program, a cooperative venture with the United States that is associated with the Strategic Defense Initiative.

Brazil

Brazil has one of the most sophisticated missile development programs in the Third World. Avibras, a Brazilian firm known for its expertise in engineering and design of aircraft and rockets, initiated the effort. In cooperation with the military, Avibras has developed a superior line of launcher hardware. The basis of the program was the development of sounding rockets, which are launched vertically and do not enter orbit.

Since it began working on military rockets in the early 1960s, Brazil has produced a large selection of products. For example, the Astros II multiple rocket launcher system, which began production in 1983, can fire three different types of rockets with ranges from nine to sixty kilometers. Such products have proved useful in earning foreign exchange and have been popular with third-world countries. The Astros II was used extensively by Iraq in its war with Iran.[25]

Brazil's space program was designed in the mid-1970s with the objective of being able to build satellites and launchers, provide launch services including a modern tracking network, and process all data. The space program plan was approved in 1979, but a key plan to collaborate with France had to be dropped due to cost. The project got underway in 1983, with funding set at one thousand million dollars.[26]

Despite dropping the French collaboration plan, Brazil's interaction with France continued. France's Arianespace launched BrazilSat 1, a Canadian-built satellite, in 1985. Meanwhile, Brazil continued to work on its own SLV capability. In 1984 Brazil successfully launched the Sonda IV rocket, which was reported to have a 174-mile range, as part of its SLV program.[27]

In 1987, the firm Orbita was established in Brazil and is believed to be in competition with Avibras.[28] Both firms are developing ballistic missiles. Avibras has worked on the SS-300, a rocket that will have a range of 300 kilometers carrying a payload of 1,000 kilograms. Also planned is the SS-1000, which will have a range of 1,000 kilometers.

Orbita meanwhile is working on the MB/EE series of missiles, which will have ranges from 150 to 1,000 kilometers.

Despite its progress, Brazil has had trouble developing liquid-propellant motors for longer range ballistic missiles and SLVs and has reportedly made an agreement with China to obtain assistance.[29] More recently, Brazil has sought assistance from France. In 1989, France made a decision to sell Viking rocket motor equipment and technology to Brazil. Although France is likely to reverse this decision, it may assist the Brazilian program piecemeal rather than through a wholesale technology transfer.

Brazil is also very willing to export military equipment. Brazil's willingness to export military equipment, generally without regard for its use, likelihood of retransfer, or other considerations, is well proven. Of all developing countries engaged in arms sales, Brazil is the second largest supplier after China.[30] Using constant 1987 dollars, it is estimated that Brazil's income from exporting arms rose from $140 million in 1977 to $600 million in 1987.[31]

India

In 1967, India began to develop sounding rockets, which became the basis for its SLV program of the 1970s. In 1980, India successfully launched a satellite using its own SLV-3, a four-stage solid-propellant system capable of carrying a forty-kilogram payload. While India's SLV program was indigenous, it benefited from a variety of imports of missile systems, components, and support technology. For example, India imported the SA-2 from the Soviet Union in the mid-1960s. The SA-2 is a two-stage surface-to-air missile that uses solid propellant in its booster stage. India's SLV program provided the technical and infrastructural basis for its ballistic missile program. In 1988, India tested its Prithvi short-range ballistic missile, a single-stage liquid-propellant system.

In May 1989, India successfully tested the two-stage Agni ballistic missile to a range exceeding 600 kilometers. The first stage uses solid propellant and is based on the SLV-3. The second stage uses liquid propellant and is a modified version of the Prithvi.

India claims to have developed its ballistic missile capabilities alone, but it has had significant outside help and continues to seek assistance. For example, India has had several contracts with the French, including one under which it purchased Viking liquid-propellant rocket motor technology. India has also relied on imported auxiliary equipment such as devices to test materials, motors, and other components. In 1988, India contracted with a U.S. firm to buy a sophisticated system to test materials under a variety of forces and temperatures, allegedly for testing related to a peaceful space program. As a result of India's test of the Agni, the U.S. government reversed itself on the licensing of this export. The Agni launch demonstrated that the Indian military ballistic missile program is inextricably intertwined with its space program.

India's next goal is to develop a polar SLV with solid-propellant rocket motors. This delivery vehicle will be able to place a 7,000-pound spacecraft in low earth orbit. Success in this effort will enable India to build intercontinental ballistic missiles. India is also interested in developing cruise missiles.

Israel

In the 1960s, in cooperation with a French firm, Israel produced Jericho, a single-stage solid-propellant missile capable of delivering a 1,000-kilogram-plus warhead to a range of more than 450 kilometers. Israel continued to improve its guidance and propulsion systems and successfully tested Jericho 2, a two-stage solid-propellant missile, to a range exceeding 800 kilometers.[32]

Israel has used its military missile program as the basis for its SLVs. The Shavit SLV is probably a Jericho 2 with an added third-stage booster. In September 1988, Israel launched its first satellite into low orbit using the Shavit. It burned up in the atmosphere when returning to earth four months later. On April 3, 1990, Israel launched its second satellite into low orbit, probably to test its effort to establish a surveillance capability.[33] This $10-million satellite is more sophisticated than the first; it can receive and respond to communications from ground control.[34]

Israel is also working with the United States on the Arrow program to develop an antitactical ballistic missile (ATBM) under the Strategic Defense Initiative. Although the Arrow is at least five years away from deployment, its development is ahead of schedule. In the meantime, the United States has agreed to lease to Israel Patriot air defense missiles and to provide intelligence from U.S. early-warning satellites to activate them.[35]

South Africa

Intense secrecy has kept the South African missile program out of the press; relatively little is publicly known about it. It is true, however, that Israel has assisted the South African missile program. Facts about the collaboration began to surface following charges brought against three South Africans for trying to export illegally American gyroscopes worth $50 million, to be used for missile guidance. One attempt to export gyroscopes reportedly involved Israel Aircraft Industries Ltd.[36]

It is clear that Israel actively seeks business that could involve missile-related technology transfer. For example, Israel Aircraft Industries placed a full-page advertisement in the April 1990 issue of the *Armed Forces Journal*. In part it said, "We've been supplying and integrating products and systems for the Israeli Defense Forces and other modern and modernizing armies for many years. We offer: Arrow ATBM."

Israel publicly denies providing South Africa with missiles, saying that it has established no new contracts since 1987, when the United States convinced it to refrain from such interactions. What is unknown is whether contracts that predated the 1987 promise were extended or amended.

Although South Africa has a high-quality infrastructure and significant experience in missile design and manufacture—it developed its own antitank missile for use in Angola—it is not likely able to develop its own intermediate-range ballistic missile. Yet in June 1989, South Africa tested such a missile at its Overberg test range outside Capetown.[37] The missile was similar to the Jericho 2.[38]

To many observers, the notion of Israeli–South African cooperation came as no surprise. A number of Israeli scientists are working in South Africa on a variety of weapons projects. For example, Israeli scientists and technicians reportedly began work on Lavi fighter aircraft in South Africa when, at American insistence, the project was shelved.

South Africa has probably been successful in importing technology directly from the United States and Western Europe as well. Details are obscure but surface occasionally. Gamma Systems Associates, a company created to smuggle high-technology items to South Africa, was discovered and reported by the press in January 1990.[39] The Gamma Systems story is complicated because multiple companies were used to hide illegal exports. Gamma was used by a second company, ESI Manufacturing, which was, in turn, used by a third firm, International

Signal and Control Group. The latter was established and run by an electrical engineer who worked for nine years for Lockheed Corporation, where he worked on at least one missile assignment. He is accused of having made millions of dollars' worth of sales to South Africa, including that of controlled missile technology.

Taiwan

The case of Taiwan is somewhat similar to that of South Africa. It is a country with a well-developed infrastructure and excellent technical capabilities, but it is dependent on foreign technology for highly sophisticated items. Also, it appears to rely on help from Israel and tries to acquire what it needs through illegal imports.

On March 1, 1988, Taiwan announced the successful testing of its Hsiung Feng II, an antiship missile. Indigenously designed and produced, it was said to be "as good as similar types of foreign missiles in terms of range, speed, target precision, and controllability."[40] It was developed by the Chung Shan Institute of Science and Technology (CIST), drawing on technology from Israel's Gabriel missile.[41] The CIST is also responsible for the surface-to-air Tien Kung I, with a 35-kilometer range, the 100-kilometer-range Tien Kung II, and the 10- to 15-kilometer-range air-to-air Tien Chien.

Any pursuit of a surface-to-surface missile by Taiwan is being kept secret. Taiwan has given the impression that it has abandoned its efforts to create the Ching Feng missile, thought by many to be modeled on the U.S. Lance, which has a range of approximately 130 kilometers. Taiwan conceivably could have obtained Lance technology from Israel, which received it from the United States.[42]

Taiwan, like other countries with ballistic missile programs, is likely to have the most trouble with guidance systems. And, like several other proliferant countries, there is some evidence that it may have illegally circumvented export controls to get the components it needs. In January 1990, TRT International of Ashland, Massachusetts, and three of its executives were indicted on federal charges of illegally exporting guidance parts for Sidewinder and Maverick missiles to Taiwan.[43] None of the sophisticated items (eleven optical receivers and three infrared domes) were recovered.[44] Although these components are not usable in ballistic missiles, Taiwan clearly tries (and sometimes succeeds) to get what it needs, even through illegal means.

North Korea

In 1969 and 1970, North Korea imported Soviet Frog-5 and Frog-7A artillery rockets. In the mid-1970s, it undertook a program to reverse engineer the Frog-7A. Shortly thereafter, it abandoned this effort to focus on research and development of a reverse-engineered version of the Scud, which it acquired from Egypt in return for help during the 1973 war in the Mideast.[45] In addition to some help from Egypt, North Korea obtained assistance from China on rocket engine design, metallurgy, and air frame technology. While it appeared that North Korea could overcome the technical challenges of upgrading and producing the Scud indigenously, the program was beset with economic difficulties.

In mid-1985, North Korea agreed to supply missile technology to Iran in return for financial support of its research and development program. Evidence of the agreement is difficult to uncover, but in October 1984 an Iranian businessman was indicted in New York for trying to export precision parts for missile guidance systems to North Korea. In January 1987, the South Korean defense minister reported that North Korea had successfully test-fired a missile at its facility north of Wonsan. Reportedly, the missile was a North Korean–produced Scud. Shortly thereafter, in June 1987, North Korea agreed to deliver up to 100 Scuds to Iran.[46]

Following successful reverse engineering of the Scud, North Korea embarked on a program to increase the standard 180- to 300-kilometer range of the missile to a 450- to 600-kilometer range. South Korean analysts have concluded that the upgraded Scud was available for deployment in late 1989.

Other Countries

It is difficult to get information about missile development programs, particularly before missiles under development have been test-fired. In addition to the programs already mentioned, there are programs in Iran, Libya, Pakistan, South Korea, and Syria about which there is little data. So little is known about Iran's missile production capabilities that rumors of its manufacturing Scuds under license[47] have not been confirmed. Iran is believed to be developing its own ballistic missile, the Iran-130, possibly with external help.

China, which has helped Iran with production of artillery rockets,[48] possibly assists Iran with its missiles. China has sold Iran its Silkworm missiles in the past, and in January 1990 signed a ten-year agreement for scientific cooperation and transfer of military technology.[49] Subsequently, China was reported to be shipping Iran M1-B surface-to-surface missiles, which had a 100-kilometer range.[50] While these missiles are short-range, the transaction is indicative of a growing relationship between the two countries. It might include technology transfer as well as hardware sales. North Korea and Iran may also have an exchange agreement.

Libya has tried to purchase ballistic missiles and technology without much success. Although it has Scuds, Libya's ability to upgrade them without outside help, from North Korea, for example, is minimal. Like Iran, Libya has been interested in Chinese missiles and technology. It would undoubtedly purchase the M-9, a 600-kilometer-range missile, if given the opportunity.

Pakistan also has a very active missile development program. Pakistan has proven its ability to make up for deficiencies in its infrastructure by using an intricate web of dummy companies, transshipment through multiple countries, and false bills-of-lading to import technology. Until recently, it has focused primarily on obtaining nuclear weapons capability, not ballistic missiles. With the 1989 Indian test of the Agni ballistic missile, this changed.

In February 1989, Pakistan claimed (without confirmation) that it had successfully tested two missiles, the 80-kilometer Hatf I and the 300-kilometer Hatf II. Like Iran and Libya, Pakistan may be seeking help from China,[51] which is known to have aided Pakistan's nuclear program and a host of other technical and military activities.

South Korea is akin to South Africa in its status and capabilities: it has a good infrastructure, significant experience with short-range missiles, and fairly strong motivations for developing longer range missiles. As mentioned, South Korea did produce an upgraded version of the U.S. Nike Hercules system, a surface-to-air missile with surface-to-surface capability. Knowing that the United States is strongly opposed to South Korea developing a ballistic missile, however, officials in Seoul would not be expected to admit whether such a program exists. This might change if the U.S.–South Korea defense relationship changes.

Syria is known to have been developing its own ballistic missile but has had serious technical problems. Like others, it has turned to outside help and is trying to buy foreign technology. Israeli military officials have stated that Syria has purchased upgraded Scuds from North Korea.[52]

In conclusion, there are a number of major missile development programs in the Third World; most seek intermediate-range capability. Some of these programs have already succeeded and others are making rapid progress. Most are rooted in experience with imported missiles and are supplemented with external help and illegally acquired components. The fact that several nonindustrialized countries are suppliers, such as Israel, China, North Korea, Argentina, means that the spread of missile technology is likely to increase.

NOTES

1. "Missile Epidemic," *The Economist,* September 23, 1989, p. 16.

2. Duncan Lennox, "The Global Proliferation of Ballistic Missiles," *Jane's Defence Weekly,* December 23, 1989, p. 1384.

3. Yi Tae-ho, "Trends and Prospects in North Korea's Guided Missile Development," *FBIS–EAS-89-228,* November 29, 1989, pp. 18–23.

4. Daniel Southerland, "China Said to Sell Missiles," *Washington Post,* March 29, 1990, p. 1.

5. Michael R. Gordon, "Beijing Avoids New Missile Sales Assurances," *New York Times,* March 30, 1990, p. 7.

6. Ibid., page 7.

7. *Jane's Defence Weekly, International Edition,* November 25, 1989, p. 1155.

8. Jim Mann, "Israeli Arms Technology Aids China," *Los Angeles Times,* June 13, 1990, p. 1.

9. Alan George, "UK Foils Iraqi Cruise Missile," *Flight International,* October 2, 1990, p. 4.

10. "U.S. Firms Reportedly Aided Iraqi Arms Effort," *Washington Post,* December 5, 1990, p. 26.

11. "2000-km Range Missiles Produced," Baghdad Voice of the Masses in Arabic, 1230 GMT, December 7, 1989, *FBIS–NES-89-235,* December 8, 1989, p. 23.

12. Office of the U.S. Secretary of Defense, "Remarks Delivered to the American Israel Public Affairs Committee," News Release No. 294-90, June 11, 1990, p. 5.

13. *Washington Times,* December 10, 1990, p. 8.

14. Bill Gertz, "Photos Show Iraqi Missile Launchers in Mauritania," *Washington Times,* May 30, 1990, p. 3.

15. Simon Fisher, "Brasilia Embarassed by Military Links," *London Financial Times,* September 18, 1990, p. 2.

16. "BBC Program on Condor Missile Development," London BBC Television Service in English, 2035 GMT, April 10, 1989, *FBIS–WEU-89-068,* April 11, 1989, pp. 4–10.

17. In addition to its work in Argentina, MBB has also been involved in Iraq's missile laboratory near Mosul.

18. Arthur F. Manfredi, Jr., et al., "Ballistic Missile Proliferation Potential of Non-major Military Powers," Congressional Research Service Report 87-654 SPR, August 6, 1987, p. 21.

19. Ibid., p. 7.

20. Andrew Slade, "Condor Project 'in Disarray,'" *Jane's Defence Weekly,* February 17, 1990, p. 295.

21. Mel Elfin, "Behind the Condor Carbon-Carbon Smuggling Scam," *US News & World Report,* July 25, 1988, p. 38.

22. "Jail Term for a Missile Crime," *New York Times International,* December 7, 1989.

23. Alan Cowell, "Cairo Aide's Ouster Tied to Effort to Get Missile Parts in U.S.," *New York Times,* April 18, 1989, p. 8.

24. Adel Darwish, "China to Update Egypt's Missiles," *Independent,* June 14, 1990, p. 2.

25. *Jane's Armour and Artillery, 1989–90,* p. 669.

26. *Jane's Spaceflight Directory, 1988–89,* p. 2.

27. Richard House, "Brazil Pursues Dreams in Space," *Washington Post,* December 13, 1984, p. F 1, 4, as cited in Manfredi et al., "Ballistic Missile Proliferation."

28. Duncan Lennox, "The Global Proliferation of Ballistic Missiles," p. 1385.

29. "DMS Market Intelligence Reports," as cited in Manfredi et al., "Ballistic Missile Proliferation."

30. U.S. Arms Control and Disarmament Agency, *World Military Expenditures and Arms Transfers, 1988,* p. 11.

31. Ibid., p. 77.

32. Martin S. Navias, "Ballistic Missile Proliferation in the Middle East," *Survival,* May/June 1989, p. 227.

33. Jackson Diehl, "Israel Launches Satellite into Surveillance Orbit," *Washington Post,* April 4, 1990, p. A35.

34. Mark Hosenball and Marie Colvin, "New Bid to Foil Arab Missiles," *London Sunday Times,* April 8, 1990, p. 19.

35. Melissa Healy, "New Anti-Missile System to Go to Israel, U.S. Says," *Los Angeles Times,* March 9, 1990, p. 1.

36. Jeff Gerth, "5 Charged in Plot to Export Arms," *New York Times International,* November 16, 1989.

37. "South African Missile Test," *Jane's Defence Weekly,* July 15, 1989, p. 59.

38. *Jane's Defence Weekly,* December 23, 1989, p. 1385.

39. Edward T. Pound and Andy Pasztor, "American Arms Dealer Was Amazing Success, or So Ferranti Believed," *Wall Street Journal,* January 23, 1990, p. 1.

40. "Long-range Antiship Missile Tested Successfully," Taipei CNA in English, 0235 GMT, March 1, 1988, *FBIS–CHI-88-040,* pp. 39–40.

41. Manfredi et al., "Ballistic Missile Proliferation," p. 44, 45.

42. Ibid.

43. *Washington Post,* January 24, 1990, p. A11.

44. Joseph A. Slobodzian, "Firm, 3 Officers Charged in Arms-Export Case," *Philadelphia Inquirer,* January 24, 1990, p. 5.

45. Yi Tai-ho, "Trends and Prospects in North Korea's Guided Missile Development," p. 21.

46. Ibid., p. 22.

47. Lennox, "The Global Proliferation of Ballistic Missiles."

48. Thomas G. Mahnken and Timothy D. Hoyt, "Missile Proliferation and American Interests," *SAIS Review,* vol. 10, no. 1, p. 105.

49. "Iran, China Sign Arms Technology Pact," *Washington Times,* January 22, 1990, p. 2.

50. Daniel Southerland, "China Said to Sell Missiles," *Washington Post,* March 29, 1990, p. 1.

51. Seth Carus, "Stopping Missile Proliferation," *The World & I,* November 1989, p. 187.

52. Jim Mann, "Syria Goes Shopping with $1 billion in Gulf Aid," *Los Angeles Times,* December 6, 1990, p. 1.

10
U.S. Policies on Missile Proliferation

The 1984 deal between Argentina, Egypt, and Iraq to develop the Condor ballistic missile alarmed the U.S. nonproliferation policy community. At the time, there was a pervasive belief that export controls were the answer to preventing missile proliferation. It was assumed that advanced missile technology was available only from the Soviet Union and the seven Western economic partners (the United States, the United Kingdom, Canada, France, Japan, West Germany, and Italy) and that banding together as an export cartel would maintain control over the technology.

The idea of using export controls was a logical one. Already there was a very effective export control regime to address the problem of nuclear proliferation. Not only were there controls placed on nuclear-related exports as a result of the Nuclear Nonproliferation Treaty (NPT), but there was an agreement between key nuclear suppliers—the so-called London Suppliers Club—that restricted even more items. It was well known that several covert nuclear weapons programs had been seriously hampered by the NPT and London Club controls. The same type of controls were sought for missile technology.

In 1985 and 1986, the United States worked with its six economic partners to develop missile export controls, resulting in the formation of the Missile Technology Control Regime (MTCR). That regime consisted of a basic policy statement, a set of guidelines to govern the conditions under which exports might occur, a list of technologies to be controlled, and an informal mechanism for sharing information among the partners. The MTCR was formally announced on April 16, 1987.

The annex listing controlled items includes two categories. Category

1 items are complete rocket systems and unmanned air vehicle systems capable of delivering a 500-kilogram or greater payload to a range of at least 300 kilometers. Production facilities and subsystems for such delivery vehicles are also included. Category 2 contains a long list of items, including propulsion components, propellants, equipment for making propellants, guidance components, flight control systems, avionics, computers, and software.

The guidelines for missile technology transfer set out several requirements:

1. All transfers will be considered on a case-by-case basis.

2. Governments will implement the guidelines in accordance with their national legislation.

3. The exporting government assumes responsibility for taking all steps necessary to ensure that the item is put only to its stated end-use.

4. The decision to transfer remains the sole and sovereign judgment of the individual government.

In evaluating whether to transfer an item contained in the annex, each partner, according to the guidelines, is to take the following factors into account:

1. Nuclear proliferation concerns;

2. Capabilities and objectives of the missile and space programs of the recipient state;

3. The significance of the transfer in terms of the potential development of nuclear weapons delivery systems other than manned aircraft;

4. The assessment of the end-use of the transfers, including the potential for retransfer;

5. The applicability of relevant multilateral agreements.

Successes of the MTCR

The MTCR was highly useful in raising international awareness of missile suppliers. The process of negotiating the MTCR not only involved intelligence sharing about the depth of the problem of missile proliferation, particularly the Condor program, but it also made partners realize that they needed to strengthen their bureaucratic organizations and mechanisms to deal with licensing of exports and with enforcement of laws. In many cases, there was not sufficient domestic legislation to outlaw exports that would be covered by the MTCR.

In the case of the United States, for example, the effort to control missile exports involves several agencies, including the Departments of Commerce, State, and Defense; the Arms Control and Disarmament Agency; and the intelligence community. Two processes are involved, one to control above-board requests for missile technology and one to address illicit attempts. In the case of the former, procedures were modeled on other export controls. With the latter, it was necessary to muster resources within the intelligence community to focus on missile proliferation and to provide the data to the policy community in a timely way. This, in turn, would allow the policymakers to contact partners and seek other means to foil any given missile export attempt. Overall, the MTCR has been responsible for a greater number of people throughout the government devoting time to missile proliferation.

In addition to providing the seven member countries with a structure and set of objectives to deal with missile proliferation, the MTCR became a model for other countries. Sweden has used MTCR guidelines as a basis for its own controls. Several countries—including Australia and members of the European Community—have indicated their desire to join the MTCR formally.

While the MTCR has succeeded in raising consciousness of the missile problem among Western suppliers and has provided a structure for export controls, its other sucesses are difficult to judge. Clearly, the Condor program of Argentina, Iraq, and Egypt has not succeeded and has been put on hold. The Condor has been set back repeatedly by the inability to import technology and equipment, which is primarily due to the effects of the MTCR. Yet the Condor has also been beset with funding problems and difficulties associated with a multinational effort involving countries of very different languages, cultures, and bureaucratic processes.

Despite the MTCR and its success in delaying or halting the Condor, missile proliferation continues at an alarming rate. Since the MTCR took effect in 1987, Saudi Arabia has imported the CSS-2 from China, India has successfully test-fired its Prithvi and Agni ballistic missiles, Israel has put a satellite into orbit, Pakistan has claimed it tested an indigenously built rocket, and Iraq has tested a four-stage satellite launch vehicle. Additionally, numerous missile development programs have been initiated around the world. So extensive and rapid are the development and spread of missile technology that the U.S. Congress passed legislation in December 1990 to try to strengthen the MTCR. Essentially the law amends the Export Administration Act to require the executive branch of the government to license almost all missile-related exports and to effect sanctions against exporters of MTCR-restricted items. The ability of this law to control missile proliferation will be only as good as the MTCR itself.

Weaknesses of the MTCR

The MTCR has several weaknesses. The first is directly related to the fact that it was a derivative of the nuclear nonproliferation regime. The MTCR is specifically designed to "control the transfer of equipment and technology that could contribute to *nuclear-capable* missiles" (emphasis added). This can be and has been interpreted as meaning that a country that does not have nuclear warheads is a suitable recipient. Thus, technically, a country that has chemical, biological, or conventional warheads is not inhibited by the MTCR. For example, the Chinese export of its CSS-2 missile to Saudi Arabia technically would not have been a violation of the MTCR guidelines even if China were an MTCR partner. This is because there is no evidence to suggest that Saudi Arabia has obtained or is trying to obtain nuclear warheads.

The United States interprets the MTCR guidelines more broadly, however. In this it differs from some of the MTCR partners. The United States points out that there is a strong "presumption of denial" for category 1 items, missiles and missile systems, which in reality means that the United States will not export such items except to close friends and allies. The United States also notes that the MTCR compels suppliers to take into consideration the capabilities and objectives of the missile and space programs of the recipient state. In its view, because space launch vehicles and ballistic missiles use the same technology, any space program is a potential military missile program.

France, for one, has disagreed with the U.S. interpretation. Its debate with the United States over the intentions underlying the MTCR highlight a second inherent problem of the MTCR: it clearly states that it is not designed to inhibit national space programs as long as the country concerned is not a nuclear proliferation risk. France has said that it will participate in the peaceful space programs of countries such as Brazil. France notes that the MTCR states that a decision to export is a sovereign one and that end-use assurances are one of the key factors a supplier must take into account. In other words, France appears willing to accept the word of an importing nation that the technology is for peaceful uses.

A third problem of the MTCR is that it is not a treaty or legal obligation. It relies on the common understanding among partners that stopping missile proliferation is more important than economic profit. In 1989, legislation was introduced in Congress to create sanctions against those caught in violation of MTCR guidelines, but Bush administration officials objected. They pointed out that the MTCR, which is not a legally binding document, recognizes that the final decision on any export belongs to the sovereign partners. The United States cannot impose its will or its interpretation.

A fourth problem with the MTCR is that its membership, although set to increase, does not and probably will not include key suppliers. China is the obvious example. The United States asked China in August 1988 to adhere to the MTCR controls, which it refused to do. China might want to avoid joining the MTCR because politically it could not afford to be viewed by the Third World as being a member of a Western condominium designed to deprive third-world nations of technology; because the United States made vast amounts of money from arms exports and China would like to do so without interference; and because China already shows restraint in its exports.

The Soviet Union's lack of participation in the MTCR also undermines the regime. During 1988–89, the U.S. government placed securing Soviet membership in the MTCR high on its list of priorities. The Soviets, however, formally declined the invitation on more than one occasion. At the heart of the Soviet response was the Scud missile, which the Soviets still export and which, with a range of 300 kilometers, would be disallowed under the MTCR. The Soviets have offered instead to build a new regime that would control missiles with very short ranges. The United States could not agree, not only because it has a vested interest in maintaining the progress already made with the MTCR, but because the Soviet suggestion would affect U.S. exports to its friends and allies.

In early 1990, the Soviet Union indicated that it would be willing to adhere to the guidelines of the MTCR, even though it would not formally join. However, the U.S.-Soviet statement on nonproliferation issued at the Bush-Gorbachev summit in late May appeared to dilute the Soviet position. While the United States sought Soviet adherence to the MTCR, the Soviets only agreed to a commitment to prevent the proliferation of "missiles and missile technologies, in particular those subject to the provisions of the Missile Technology Control

Regime." It is still possible that the Soviet Union will change its mind and join.

China and the Soviet Union are not the only non-MTCR suppliers of missile technology. Israel has worked with South Africa on ballistic missile development and has cooperated with Taiwan as well. North Korea, which reportedly reverse engineered and now produces the Scud, could export that type of missile. And it is not known how much technology has been transferred from Argentina to its Condor partners, Iraq and Egypt. In the future, as nations develop their capabilities, as India has, will they seek to export missiles and related technology? They certainly may, if motivated by economics or politics.

Another weakness of the MTCR as a means to fight missile proliferation is that it does nothing to dampen the motivations of nations seeking ballistic missiles for military purposes. The MTCR is a means of limiting supply but not demand.

In the nuclear nonproliferation regime, nations can sign treaties to signal their political decision to refrain from acquiring nuclear weapons. While there are no guarantees, the act of signing such a treaty creates a political barrier to proliferation. Another important attribute of the nuclear nonproliferation regime is the existence of safeguards, which are a technical means of verifying that specific nuclear materials and facilities are not being used for nonpeaceful purposes. In the missile nonproliferation regime, there are no parallels.

The INF Answer

One way to improve the missile nonproliferation regime is to create a treaty banning key delivery systems. A model for such a treaty is provided by the U.S.-Soviet Intermediate Nuclear Forces Treaty (INF). Under INF, the United States and the Soviet Union banned all ground-launched intermediate-range ballistic missiles (500–5,500 kilometers). Other nations should be called upon to match this arms control achievement.

An international INF treaty should not substitute for or interfere in any way with the bilateral INF treaty, which has special provisions that deal with U.S. and Soviet forces, the destruction of specific missiles, and other issues that apply only to these two states. Likewise, the introduction of an international INF treaty should not make the bilateral treaty subject to renegotiation or even the slightest alteration. Nor should an international treaty place requirements on other nations that would not apply to the superpowers as well.

Publicly Refute Reasons for Indigenous SLVs

Even if there were a global ban on INF-range missiles, there would still be a need to deter development of intercontinental ballistic missiles. The most likely way a nation would go about developing ICBMs is to do so under the guise of establishing an indigenous satellite launch vehicle program. Even if an SLV is developed with civil applications in mind, a country could later decide to apply the technology to a ballistic missile program. One way to prevent missile proliferation via SLV programs is to provide the public with reasons why an indigenous SLV program is impractical. The public needs data to show that:

• Domestic SLV programs are incredibly expensive and risky;
• There are SLV services available at reasonable costs;
• The technology of indigenous programs will be obsolete in comparison with advanced countries' services;
• Intelligence data are already available.

Independent SLV programs by less-developed countries do not make economic sense. Duplicating the research, experimentation, and construction already accomplished by several industrialized nations would cost billions of dollars. The alternative—using the satellite construction and launch services already available—is cheap by comparison.

It is also important for the public to be aware that the financial costs of an SLV do not necessarily end with completion of research, development, and construction. Even if a country does invest the resources to develop an SLV, the risk of serious financial loss remains high. Martin Marietta, a U.S. company with significant high-level technology experience, provides a good example. The company suffered serious losses in its fledgling commercial space delivery services program on March 14, 1990, when it set an Intelsat 6 communications satellite in an unusable low orbit because of a launch vehicle problem. Losses were estimated at $265 million, of which $115 million were launch costs.

In part, the problem could have been due to inexperience; the launch was only the company's second. But other companies with extensive experience have had similar accidents. France's Arianespace suffered a comparable loss when its Ariane 44L SLV, with two Japanese satellites worth $240 million aboard, exploded after liftoff on February

22, 1990. This happened despite Arianespace's extensive experience; it had had seventeen successful launches prior to the accident. Of the thirty-seven satellite launches between 1979 and September 1990, Arianespace suffered five failures.[1]

The Soviet Union also has had problems. On October 4, 1990, the Soviet Zenit booster—an advanced booster rocket being promoted for sale abroad—exploded just after liftoff, destroying much of the launch pad. Although no figures on the cost of damage were released, there is no doubt that the financial blow was severe. The booster, its payload, the launch pad, and perhaps potential business for the Zenit were lost.

In addition to financial losses, there can be loss of life as well. This is particularly true in the early stages of a rocket launch program, when safety procedures might not be as well developed. The Soviet Union lost 165 people, including a top general, when a rocket blew up on the launch pad at Baikonur Space Center in October 1960.[2]

In addition to the financial costs and other risks associated with launches, there are significant costs in keeping SLV and satellite technology up to date. The rapid advances in satellite and launch technology virtually assure that a less-developed country's SLV efforts will be obsolete in no time. Advanced satellites need to be high powered, particularly as ground stations are made smaller. This means that there is a push to reduce the cost per watt of power that a satellite transmits. Because satellite launch costs are about half of the satellite segment costs and these vary with weight, the emphasis is for the maximum number of watts per pound of launch weight.[3] Electric power systems, transmitters, and propulsion systems are the main factors in satellite weight, meaning that increasingly sophisticated technology must be used to reduce the weight of satellites.

One product of advanced technology that is used to make satellites lighter and therefore less costly to launch is the electrical thruster, a motor that does not rely on a heavy propellant to provide energy. Since about one-half of a spacecraft's launch mass is propellant, the use of electrical thrusters, which are more efficient than conventional chemical rockets, can significantly lighten the load. However, electrical thrusters are very complicated engineering challenges.

In summary, an effort should be made to inform the media, business community, and decision-making elites in countries developing SLVs of the risks, financial costs, probability of technological inferiority, and lack of necessity of their country's SLV efforts. These groups should also be made aware that SLV technology could be diverted to ballistic missiles. Given these data, some countries might be forced to reconsider whether SLV development is the best way to spend scarce resources.

Provide Launch Services

Nations that want the benefits of satellites will work to acquire them, and developed countries should assist them in their quest. It can be argued that satellite construction and launch services have not been made available to many countries in a timely manner or at a reasonable cost. If they were, it is unlikely that some of the nations considering indigenous programs would incur the cost.

The countries thus far responsible for commercial space development have been interested in large satellites, which involve great cost. As reported in *Aviation Week & Space Technology,* "McDonnell Douglas' Delta rocket can put 4,100 pounds of payload in geosynchronous orbit for $50 million. General Dynamics' Atlas Centaur can throw about 8,000 pounds that far for $65 million. And Martin Marietta's monster Titan can lift more than three times that weight for $80 million. But entrepreneurs who envisioned uses for lighter and lower-orbiting satellites were forced to ride second class behind a bigger project on a big, expensive rocket."[4]

Fortunately, this is likely to change. The U.S. Pegasus is a booster rocket that resembles a large cruise missile and is launched from the underwing pylon of a B-52 bomber. It will be able to place a 900-pound satellite into equatorial or polar orbit at a cost of $7–8 million. Technologists are working to make the Pegasus capable of delivering payload into geosynchronous orbit as well.

The United States is not the only country working to fill the need for satellites and launch services. Arianespace, for example, plans to begin a microsatellite (50 kilograms or less) launch service. One launch, carrying up to six microsatellites, will cost $600,000. Thus, a country could use this SLV for as little as $100,000. A minisat (400 to 1000 kilograms) launch service planned by Arianespace is slated to cost only $16–24 million.[5]

If commercial firms do begin to offer satellite services at lower cost, it surely will influence countries whose SLV programs are under development. For those countries it would be economically reasonable to set aside indigenous efforts and ride with Pegasus or Arianespace.

"Open Skies" Should Be Tried

One reason that a country may choose to develop its own SLV program despite the costs and likelihood of technological obsolescence is to obtain intelligence. Many countries that feel threatened would like access to photointelligence, which would provide them information on the location and activities of a potential enemy's military forces.

President Dwight D. Eisenhower suggested a policy of "open skies" at the 1955 Geneva summit. Since then, NATO and Warsaw Pact countries have accepted the notion of allowing aircraft to fly over their countries on a regular basis to provide information on activities of potential threat or concern in the subject country. Although open skies negotiations have been stalled by Soviet demands for tight controls over the aircraft and their routes, the principle could be used in other regions of the world. This type of policy would be particularly useful for countries that traditionally have been at odds and may be engaged in an arms race. An open skies agreement could serve to reduce tensions and build confidence during peacetime. Obviously, if hostilities appear imminent, open skies would not be workable.

If satellite imagery is available to only one party in a potential conflict, the other party is obviously disadvantaged. Such a situation can promote rather than dampen instability. In the case of the Middle East, Israel's development of SLVs and its proven ability to build and orbit satellites has placed Arab states on the defensive. Iraq, for example, has responded with its own crash program to build an SLV and will undoubtedly pursue satellite-gathered intelligence capability.

To avoid imbalances in satellite imagery capability, the concept of open skies should be extended to all regions of the world, perhaps via a plan to make satellite imagery available to all. To some extent, this is already happening. Imagery from satellites useful for observing military facilities and activities is commercially available. While the imagery is not of a sufficiently high resolution to permit precise target descriptions, the data are probably cheaper and of better quality than any that could be collected by a country with relatively low satellite design capabilities.

The French SPOT satellite, for example, has been in orbit since February 1986. It provides imagery with a resolution of ten meters and can be stereoscopic. SPOT imagery of any site on earth can be ordered by anyone, as long as the target area is not in or near a war zone. (For example, SPOT officials suspended open sales of Middle East coverage when Iraq invaded Kuwait and the international community began a military buildup in defense of Saudi Arabia.) A SPOT digital tape can be purchased for $2,200 to $3,500, which is not much when compared with the cost of designing, building, deploying, and operating a reconnaisance satellite.

France is not the only supplier of such imagery. In 1992, Japan will launch an earth-sensing satellite with a resolution of eighteen meters and a synthetic aperture radar that permits penetration of clouds and darkness. Even the Soviets are preparing to enter the market. One product, imaging data from Soviet Almaz radar reconnaisance remote sensing platforms, will have a resolution of fifteen to twenty-five meters. The twenty-four-by-twenty-four mile scenes from the satellite will be marketed for about $1,600 each by Space Commerce Corporation, a U.S. Firm in partnership with the Soviet space agency Glavkosmos.[6]

In the future, there may also be a multinational source for satellite data and, equally important, analysis services. The nine-member Western European Union agreed to develop satellite reconnaisance capability for the purpose of verifying cuts in conventional forces in Europe.[7] Once it is operational, perhaps such an organization can provide data and analyses to others.

One potential problem is the possibility of misreading the data. As Hugh DeSantis has written, "Photo interpretation, like other aspects of intelligence analysis, is not an exact science, and arguments among skilled photo analysts are quite common. Developing countries that lack expertise in photo interpretation and a data base against which to evaluate satellite imagery are more likely to make errors."[8] It would therefore be beneficial for the United States and other countries with experience in imagery analysis to provide assistance. It might also be useful for countries in a region or grouping to pool their resources to provide their own photoanalysis capability.

In conclusion, international sources of satellite-gathered intelligence will offer nations an alternative to developing an independent SLV for reconnaisance satellite purposes. Photo misinterpretation can be reduced by international assistance and multinational analytical efforts. Stemming the development of SLVs will prevent the danger of this technology being turned to missile launching purposes.

NOTES

1. Jacques Neher, "In the March to Space, Europeans Prove They Can Muster Unity," *International Herald Tribune,* September 3, 1990, p. 17.

2. "Army Paper Says 165 Died in 1960 Rocket Accident," *Baltimore Sun,* October 25, 1990, p. 9.

3. "On a Wing and $60 Million," *Washington Times,* April 30, 1990, p. F2.

4. "Arianespace Expects to Sign New Launch Contracts Despite V36 Launch Failure," *Aviation Week & Space Technology,* March 19, 1990, p. 191.

5. Michael A. Dornheim, "Mass Market for Satellites to Be Tested Over Next Decade," *Aviation Week & Space Technology,* March 19, 1990, p. 189.

6. "Soviets to Sell High-Resolution Satellite Radar Images, Data," *Aerospace Daily,* September 17, 1990, p. 443.

7. Theresa Hitchens, "WEU Hopes to Create Satellite Agency for Treaty Verification," *Defense News,* November 20, 1989, p. 46.

8. Hugh De Santis, "Commercial Observation Satellites and Their Military Implications: A Speculative Assessment," *The Washington Quarterly,* Summer 1989, p. 197.

Conclusion

The first draft of this manuscript had just been completed when Iraq invaded and occupied Kuwait in the summer of 1990. The event confirmed for the world Iraq's possession of chemical weapons, biological weapons, and ballistic missiles. Perhaps more important to Western Europe and the United States, the invasion demonstrated that Iraq's horrendous capabilities could directly threaten Western interests as well as troops sent to protect Saudi Arabia from Iraqi ambitions. It must be noted that the industrialized nations of the world had not been unduly concerned when these Iraqi weapons were used earlier against Iran, a country that had tarnished its own image by its hostage taking and hostility.

Iraq's President, Saddam Hussein, tried repeatedly to shift at least some of the international attention and concern to Israel. He even offered to eliminate Iraq's weapons of mass destruction if Israel were required to do the same. The idea that Iraq would give up chemical and biological weapons in exchange for Israel giving up its nuclear weapons is intriguing but impractical, for the ample capabilities of others such as Iran, Syria, Egypt, Libya, and Saudi Arabia would remain intact. And that simply cannot be. Whatever settlement takes place to get rid of weapons of mass destruction must involve a pact between all the regional states.

The interrelationship of the "four proliferations" in the Middle East should teach U.S. policymakers that the problem must be treated in an integrated fashion. There should not be a policy for nuclear proliferation separate from that of missile or chemical or biological proliferation. This does not mean that policy tools that address only one of the four—such as the NPT or the MTCR—should be abandoned. Rather, these tools as well as policies and procedures that address all four kinds of weapons at once should be considered necessary.

Just as nuclear proliferation policies should not be treated in isolation from chemical proliferation problems, and so on, the proliferation phenomenon as a whole should not be isolated from foreign policy. By passing laws that treated the Pakistani nuclear proliferation problem separately from other foreign policy interests, the United States put itself in a bind and ultimately found that there are times when greater value must be placed on broader foreign policy interests than on specific proliferation activities by one nation. As a result, U.S. policy toward Pakistan appeared as impotent as it was.

Arms control and nonproliferation policies should be carefully integrated with other foreign policies. Though one might think such is already the case, it has not been so in the recent past. The U.S. Department of State has now, and has had for some time, a special ambassador for nuclear nonproliferation. This ambassador does not have responsibility for any of the other arms proliferation issues, nor for any of the myriad foreign policy issues. The assistant secretaries who deal with bilateral and "country-related" issues do not focus on nuclear proliferation, knowing that this sensitive issue is someone else's responsibility. They often do not deal in any in-depth way with chemical, biological, or missile proliferation either because these are to some extent the provinces of export controllers and of the arms control community. Thus, some of the people who know the countries, personalities, and problems of a region best are not engaged in trying to solve the proliferation problem.

There is an intense need to treat the problem of proliferation as seriously as, for example, U.S.-Soviet arms control. In the United States, there are a host of experts working on superpower arms control—not only country specialists, but individuals well versed in arms control issues. The same needs to happen for proliferation arms control policy.

Notice that *arms control,* not export control, is called for. The United States and other countries cannot afford to continue to believe that export controls alone will do the job. In this book I have sought to describe how easy or difficult proliferation is and how widespread the phenomenon is becoming. Proliferation, as shown, is occurring despite export controls. Granted, export controls can be tightened, but there will always be a supplier to meet a particular demand as long as that demand exists. As with the drug supply problem, as soon as one source is stymied, another crops up because the price is alluring. The same will happen with technologies and materials for weapons of mass destruction. We must find a way to lessen the demand, not just to limit the supply.

Although the ideas I set out for new initiatives on arms control are not complete, they do provide a starting point. Whatever is done, however, must be done in concert with other nations. Attempts by Congress to legislate missile nonproliferation are unilateral acts that can seriously damage multilateral efforts. The United States cannot succeed in meeting the arms control challenge on its own. Most important, initiatives must involve those countries that have the most to lose from proliferation—namely, the nations that are pursuing weapons of mass destruction.

Appendix
1

Protocol for the Prohibition of the Use in War of Asphyxiating, Poisonous, or Other Gases, and of Bacteriological Methods of Warfare

Signed at Geneva June 17, 1925
Entered into force February 8, 1928
Ratification advised by the U.S. Senate December 16, 1974
Ratified by U.S. President January 22, 1975
U.S. ratification deposited with the Government of France April 10, 1975
Proclaimed by U.S. President April 29, 1975

The Undersigned Plenipotentiaries, in the name of their respective Governments:

Whereas the use in war of asphyxiating, poisonous or other gases, and of all analogous liquids, materials or devices, has been justly condemned by the general opinion of the civilized world; and

Whereas the prohibition of such use has been declared in Treaties to which the majority of Powers of the World are Parties; and

To the end that this prohibition shall be universally accepted as a part of International Law, binding alike the conscience and the practice of nations;

Declare:

That the High Contracting Parties, so far as they are not already Parties to Treaties prohibiting such use, accept this prohibition, agree to extend this prohibition to the use of bacteriological methods of warfare and agree to be bound as between themselves according to the terms of this declaration.

The High Contracting Parties will exert every effort to induce other States to accede to the present Protocol. Such accession will be notified to the Government of the French Republic, and by the latter to all signatory and acceding Powers, and will take effect on the date of the notification by the Government of the French Republic.

The present Protocol, of which the French and English texts are both authentic, shall be ratified as soon as possible. It shall bear today's date.

The ratifications of the present Protocol shall be addressed to the Government of the French Republic, which will at once notify the deposit of such ratification to each of the signatory and acceding Powers.

The instruments of ratification of and accession to the present Protocol will remain deposited in the archives of the Government of the French Republic.

The present Protocol will come into force for each signatory Power as from the date of deposit of its ratification, and, from that moment, each Power will be bound as regards other powers which have already deposited their ratifications.

IN WITNESS WHEREOF the Plenipotentiaries have signed the present Protocol.

DONE at Geneva in a single copy, this seventeenth day of June, One Thousand Nine Hundred and Twenty-Five.

Appendix
2

Treaty on the Nonproliferation
of Nuclear Weapons

Signed at Washington, London, and Moscow July 1, 1968
Ratification advised by U.S. Senate March 13, 1969
Ratified by U.S. President November 24, 1969
U.S. ratification deposited at Washington, London, and Moscow March
5, 1970
Proclaimed by U.S. President March 5, 1970
Entered into force March 5, 1970

The States concluding this Treaty, hereinafter referred to as the "Parties to the Treaty",

Considering the devastation that would be visited upon all mankind by a nuclear war and the consequent need to make every effort to avert the danger of such a war and to take measures to safeguard the security of peoples,

Believing that the proliferation of nuclear weapons would seriously enhance the danger of nuclear war,

In conformity with resolutions of the United Nations General Assembly calling for the conclusion of an agreement on the prevention of wider dissemination of nuclear weapons,

Undertaking to cooperate in facilitating the application of International Atomic Energy Agency safeguards on peaceful nuclear activities,

Expressing their support for research, development and other efforts to further the application, within the framework of the International Atomic Energy Agency safeguards system, of the principle of safeguarding effectively the flow of source and special fissionable materials by use of instruments and other techniques at certain strategic points,

Affirming the principle that the benefits of peaceful applications of nuclear technology, including any technological by-products which may be derived by nuclear-weapon States from the development of nuclear explosive devices, should be available for peaceful purposes to all Parties of the Treaty, whether nuclear-weapon or non-nuclear weapon States,

Convinced that, in furtherance of this principle, all Parties to the Treaty are entitled to participate in the fullest possible exchange of scientific information for, and to contribute alone or in cooperation with other States to, the further development of the applications of atomic energy for peaceful purposes,

Declaring their intention to achieve at the earliest possible date the cessation of the nuclear arms race and to undertake effective measures in the direction of nuclear disarmament,

Urging the cooperation of all States in the attainment of this objective,

Recalling the determination expressed by the Parties to the 1963 Treaty banning nuclear weapon tests in the atmosphere, in outer space and under water in its Preamble to seek to achieve the discontinuance of all test explosions of nuclear weapons for all time and to continue negotiations to this end,

Desiring to further the easing of international tension and the strengthening of trust between States in order to facilitate the cessation of the manufacture of nuclear weapons, the liquidation of all their existing stockpiles, and the elimination from national arsenals of nuclear weapons and the means of their delivery pursuant to a treaty on general and complete disarmament under strict and effective international control,

Recalling that, in accordance with the Charter of the United Nations, States must refrain in their international relations from the threat or use of force against the territorial integrity or political independence of any State, or in any other manner inconsistent with the Purposes of the United Nations, and that the establishment and maintenance of international peace and security are to be promoted with the least diversion for armaments of the world's human and economic resources,

Have agreed as follows:

Article I

Each nuclear-weapon State Party to the Treaty undertakes not to transfer to any recipient whatsoever nuclear weapons or other nuclear explosive devices or control over such weapons or explosive devices directly, or indirectly; and not in any way to otherwise acquire nuclear weapons or other nuclear explosive devices, or control over such weapons or explosive devices.

Article II

Each non-nuclear-weapon State Party to the Treaty undertakes not to receive the transfer from any transfer or whatsoever of nuclear weapons or other nuclear explosive devices or of control over such weapons or explosive devices directly, or indirectly; not to manufacture or otherwise acquire nuclear weapons or other nuclear explosive devices; and not to seek or receive any assistance in the manufacture of nuclear weapons or other nuclear explosive devices.

Article III

1. Each non-nuclear-weapon State Party to the Treaty undertakes to accept safeguards, as set forth in an agreement to be negotiated and concluded with the International Atomic Energy Agency in accordance with the Statute of the International Atomic Energy Agency and the Agency's safeguards system, for the exclusive purpose of verification of the fulfillment of its obligations assumed under this Treaty with a view to preventing diversion of nuclear energy from peaceful uses to nuclear weapons or other nuclear explosive devices. Procedures for the safeguards required by this article shall be followed with respect to source or special fissionable material whether it is being produced, processed or used in any principal nuclear facility or is outside any such facility. The safeguards required by this article shall be applied to all source or special fissionable material in all peaceful nuclear activities within the territory of such State, under its jurisdiction, or carried out under its control anywhere.

2. Each State Party to the Treaty undertakes not to provide: (a) source or special fissionable material, or (b) equipment or material especially designed or prepared for the processing, use or production of special fissionable material, to any non-nuclear-weapon State for peaceful purposes, unless the source or special fissionable material shall be subject to the safeguards required by this article.

3. The safeguards required by this article shall be implemented

in a manner designed to comply with article IV of this Treaty, and to avoid hampering the economic or technological development of the Parties or international cooperation in the field of peaceful nuclear activities, including the international exchange of nuclear material and equipment for the processing, use or production of nuclear material for peaceful purposes in accordance with the provisions of this article and the principle of safeguarding set forth in the Preamble of the Treaty.

4. Non-nuclear-weapon States Party to the Treaty shall conclude agreements with the International Atomic Energy Agency to meet the requirements of this article either individually or together with other States in accordance with the Statute of the International Atomic Energy Agency. Negotiation of such agreements shall commence within 180 days from the original entry into force of this Treaty. For States depositing their instruments of ratification or accession after the 180-day period, negotiation of such agreements shall commence not later than the date of such deposit. Such agreements shall enter into force not later than eighteen months after the date of initiation of negotiations.

Article IV

1. Nothing in this Treaty shall be interpreted as affecting the inalienable right of all the Parties to the Treaty to develop research, production and use of nuclear energy for peaceful purposes without discrimination and in conformity with articles I and II of this Treaty.

2. All the Parties to the Treaty undertake to facilitate, and have the right to participate in, the fullest possible exchange of equipment, materials and scientific and technological information for the peaceful uses of nuclear energy. Parties to the Treaty in a position to do so shall also cooperate in contributing alone or together with other States or international organizations to the further development of the applications of nuclear energy for peaceful purposes, especially in the territories of non-nuclear-weapon States Party to the Treaty, with due consideration for the needs of the developing areas of the world.

Article V

Each party to the Treaty undertakes to take appropriate measures to ensure that, in accordance with this Treaty, under appropriate international observation and through appropriate international procedures, potential benefits from any peaceful applications of nuclear explosions will be made available to non-nuclear-weapon States Party to the Treaty on a nondiscriminatory basis and that the charge to such Parties for the explosive devices used will be as low as possible and exclude any charge for research and development. Non-nuclear-weapon States Party to the Treaty shall be able to obtain such benefits, pursuant to a special international agreement or agreements, through an appropriate international body with adequate representation of non-nuclear-weapon States. Negotiations on this subject shall commence as soon as possible after the Treaty enters into force. Non-nuclear-weapon States Party to the Treaty so desiring may also obtain such benefits pursuant to bilateral agreements.

Article VI

Each of the Parties to the Treaty undertakes to pursue negotiations in good faith on effective measures relating to cessation of the nuclear arms race at an early date and to nuclear disarmament, and on a treaty on general and complete disarmament under strict and effective international control.

Article VII

Nothing in this Treaty affects the right of any group of States to conclude regional treaties in order to assure the total absence of nuclear weapons in their respective territories.

Article VIII

1. Any Party to the Treaty may propose amendments to this Treaty. The text of any proposed amendment shall be submitted to the Depositary Governments which shall circulate it to all Parties to the Treaty. Thereupon, if requested to do so by one-third or more of the Parties to

the Treaty, the Depositary Governments shall convene a conference, to
which they shall invite all the Parties to the Treaty, to consider such an
amendment.

2. Any amendment to this Treaty must be approved by a majority of
the votes of all the Parties to the Treaty, including the votes of all
nuclear-weapon States Party to the Treaty and all other Parties which,
on the date the amendment is circulated, are members of the Board of
Governors of the International Atomic Energy Agency. The amendment shall enter into force for each Party that deposits its instrument of
ratification of the amendment upon the deposit of such instruments of
ratification by a majority of all the Parties, including the instruments of
ratification of all nuclear-weapon States Party to the Treaty and all other
Parties which, on the date the amendment is circulated, are members of
the Board of Governors of the International Atomic Energy Agency.
Thereafter, it shall enter into force for any other Party upon the deposit
of its instrument of ratification of the amendment.

3. Five years after the entry into force of this Treaty, a conference of
Parties to the Treaty shall be held in Geneva, Switzerland, in order to
review the operation of this Treaty with a view to assuring that the
purposes of the Preamble and the provisions of the Treaty are being
realized. At intervals of five years thereafter, a majority of the Parties to
the Treaty may obtain, by submitting a proposal to this effect to the
Depositary Governments, the convening of further conferences with
the same objective of reviewing the operation of the Treaty.

Article IX

1. This Treaty shall be open to all States for signature. Any State
which does not sign the Treaty before its entry into force in accordance
with paragraph 3 of this article may accede to it at any time.

2. This Treaty shall be subject to ratification by signatory States.
Instruments of ratification and instruments of accession shall be deposited
with the Governments of the United States of America, the United
Kingdom of Great Britain and Northern Ireland and the Union of
Soviet Socialist Republics, which are hereby designated the Depositary
Governments.

3. This Treaty shall enter into force after its ratification by the
State, the Governments of which are designated Depositaries of the
Treaty, and forty other States signatory to this Treaty and the deposit of

their instruments of ratification. For the purposes of this Treaty, a nuclear-weapon State is one which has manufactured and exploded a nuclear weapon or other nuclear explosive device prior to January 1, 1967.

4. For States whose instruments of ratification or accession are deposited subsequent to the entry into force of this Treaty, it shall enter into force on the date of the deposit of their instruments of ratification or accession.

5. The Depositary Governments shall promptly inform all signatory and acceding States of the date of each signature, the date of deposit of each instrument of ratification or of accession, the date of the entry into force of this Treaty, and the date of receipt of any requests for convening a conference or other notices.

6. This Treaty shall be registered by the Depositary Governments pursuant to article 102 of the Charter of the United Nations.

Article X

1. Each Party shall in exercising its national sovereignty have the right to withdraw from the Treaty if it decides that extraordinary events, related to the subject matter of this Treaty, have jeopardized the supreme interests of its country. It shall give notice of such withdrawal to all other Parties to the Treaty and to the United Nations Security Council three months in advance. Such notice shall include a statement of the extraordinary events it regards as having jeopardized its supreme interests.

2. Twenty-five years after the entry into force of the Treaty, a conference shall be convened to decide whether the Treaty shall continue in force indefinitely, or shall be extended for an additional fixed period or periods. This decision shall be taken by a majority of the Parties to the Treaty.

Article XI

This Treaty, the English, Russian, French, Spanish and Chinese texts of which are equally authentic, shall be deposited in the archives of the Depositary Governments. Duly certified copies of this Treaty shall be transmitted by the Depositary Governments to the Governments of the signatory and acceding States.

IN WITNESS WHEREOF the undersigned, duly authorized, have signed this Treaty.

DONE in triplicate, at the cities of Washington, London, and Moscow, this first day of July one thousand nine hundred sixty-eight.

Appendix

3

Convention on the Prohibition of the Development, Production, and Stockpiling of Bacteriological (Biological) and Toxin Weapons and on Their Destruction

Signed at Washington, London, and Moscow April 10, 1972
Ratification advised by U.S. Senate December 16, 1974
Ratified by U.S. President January 22, 1975
U.S. ratification deposited at Washington, London, and Moscow March 26, 1975
Proclaimed by U.S. President March 26, 1975
Entered into force March 26, 1975

The States Parties to this Convention,

Determined to act with a view to achieving effective progress towards general and complete disarmament, including the prohibition and elimination of all types of weapons of mass destruction, and convinced that the prohibition of the development, production and stockpiling of chemical and bacteriological (biological) weapons and their elimination, through effective measures, will facilitate the achievement of general and complete disarmament under strict and effective international control,

Recognizing the important significance of the Protocol for the Prohibition of the Use in War of Asphyxiating, Poisonous or Other Gases, and of Bacteriological Methods of Warfare, signed at Geneva on June 17, 1925, and conscious also of the contribution which the said Protocol has already made, and continues to make, to mitigating the horrors of war,

Reaffirming their adherence to the principles and objectives of that Protocol and calling upon all States to comply strictly with them,

Recalling that the General Assembly of the United Nations has repeatedly condemned all actions contrary to the principles and objectives of the Geneva Protocol of June 17, 1925.

Desiring to contribute to the strengthening of confidence between peoples and the general improvement of the international atmosphere,

Desiring also to contribute to the realization of the purposes and principles of the Charter of the United Nations.

Convinced of the importance and urgency of eliminating from the arsenals of States, through effective measures, such dangerous weapons of mass destruction as those using chemical or bacteriological (biological) agents.

Recognizing that an agreement on the prohibition of bacteriological (biological) and toxin weapons represents a first possible step towards the achievement of agreement on effective measures also for the prohibition of the development, production and stockpiling of chemical weapons, and determined to continue negotiations to that end,

Determined, for the sake of all mankind, to exclude completely the possibility of bacteriological (biological) agents and toxins being used as weapons,

Convinced that such use would be repugnant to the conscience of mankind and that no effort should be spared to minimize this risk,

Have agreed as follows:

Article I

Each State Party to this Convention undertakes never in any circumstances to develop, produce, stockpile or otherwise acquire or retain:

(1) Microbial or other biological agents, or toxins whatever their origin or method of production, of types and in quantities that have no justification for prophylactic, protective or other peaceful purposes;

(2) Weapons, equipment or means of delivery designed to use such agents or toxins for hostile purposes or in armed conflict.

Article II

Each State Party to this Convention undertakes to destroy, or to divert to peaceful purposes, as soon as possible but not later than nine months after the entry into force of the Convention, all agents, toxins, weapons, equipment and means of delivery specified in article I of the Convention, which are in its possession or under its jurisdiction or control. In implementing the provisions of this article all necessary safety precautions shall be observed to protect populations and the environment.

Article III

Each State Party to this Convention undertakes not to transfer to any recipient whatsoever, directly or indirectly, and not in any way to assist, encourage, or induce any State, group of States or international organizations to manufacture or otherwise acquire any of the agents, toxins, weapons, equipment or means of delivery specified in article I of the Convention.

Article IV

Each State Party to this Convention shall, in accordance with its constitutional processes, take any necessary measures to prohibit and prevent the development, production, stockpiling, acquisition, or retention of the agents, toxins, weapons, equipment and means of delivery specified in article I of the Convention, within the territory of such State, under its jurisdiction or under its control anywhere.

Article V

The States Parties to this Convention undertake to consult one another and to cooperate in solving any problems which may arise in relation to the objective of, or in the application of the provisions of, the Convention. Consultation and cooperation pursuant to this article may also be undertaken through appropriate international procedures within the framework of the United Nations and in accordance with its Charter.

Article VI

(1) Any State Party to this Convention which finds that any other State Party is acting in breach of obligations deriving from the provisions of the Convention may lodge a complaint with the Security

Council of the United Nations. Such a complaint should include all possible evidence confirming its validity, as well as a request for its consideration by the Security Council.

(2) Each State Party to this Convention undertakes to cooperate in carrying out any investigation which the Security Council may initiate, in accordance with the provisions of the Charter of the United Nations, on the basis of the complaint received by the Council. The Security Council shall inform the States Parties to the Convention of the results of the investigation.

Article VII

Each State Party to this Convention undertakes to provide or support assistance, in accordance with the United Nations Charter, to any Party to the Convention which so requests, if the Security Council decides that such Party has been exposed to danger as a result of violation of the Convention.

Article VIII

Nothing in this Convention shall be interpreted as in any way limiting or detracting from the obligations assumed by any State under the Protocol for the Prohibition of the Use in War of Asphyxiating, Poisonous or Other Gases, and of Bacteriological Methods of Warfare, signed at Geneva on June 17, 1925.

Article IX

Each State Party to this Convention affirms the recognized objective of effective prohibition of chemical weapons and, to this end, undertakes to continue negotiations in good faith with a view to reaching early agreement on effective measures for the prohibition of their development, production and stockpiling and for their destruction, and on appropriate measures concerning equipment and means of delivery specifically designed for the production or use of chemical agents for weapons purposes.

Article X

(1) The States Parties to this Convention undertake to facilitate, and have the right to participate in, the fullest possible exchange of equipment, materials and scientific and technological information for the use of bacteriological (biological) agents and toxins for peaceful purposes. Parties to the Convention in a position to do so shall also cooperate in contributing individually or together with other States or international organizations to the further development and application of scientific discoveries in the field of bacteriology (biology) for prevention of disease, or for other peaceful purposes.

(2) This Convention shall be implemented in a manner designed to avoid hampering the economic or technological development of States Parties to the Convention or international cooperation in the field of peaceful bacteriological (biological) activities, including the international exchange of bacteriological (biological) agents and toxins and equipment for the processing, use or production of bacteriological (biological) agents and toxins for peaceful purposes in accordance with the provisions of the Convention.

Article XI

Any State Party may propose amendments to this Convention. Amendments shall enter into force for each State Party accepting the amendments upon their acceptance by a majority of the States Parties to the Convention and thereafter for each remaining State Party on the date of acceptance by it.

Article XII

Five years after the entry into force of this Convention, or earlier if it is requested by a majority of Parties to the Convention by submitting a proposal to this effect to the Depositary Governments, a conference of States Parties to the Convention shall be held at Geneva, Switzerland, to review the operation of the Convention, with a view to assuring that the purposes of the preamble and the provisions of the Convention, including the provisions concerning negotiations on chemical weapons, are being realized. Such review shall take into account any new scientific and technological developments relevant to the Convention.

Article XIII

(1) This Convention shall be of unlimited duration.

(2) Each State Party to this Convention shall in exercising its national sovereignty have the right to withdraw from the Convention if it decides that extraordinary events, related to the subject matter of the Convention, have jeopardized the supreme interests of its country. It shall give notice of such withdrawal to all other States Parties to the Convention and to the United Nations Security Council three months in advance. Such notice shall include a statement of the extraordinary events it regards as having jeopardized its supreme interests.

Article XIV

(1) This Convention shall be open to all States for signature. Any State which does not sign the Convention before its entry into force in accordance with paragraph (3) of this Article may accede to it at any time.

(2) This Convention shall be subject to ratification by signatory States. Instruments of ratification and instruments of accession shall be deposited with the Governments of the United States of America, the United Kingdom of Great Britain and Northern Ireland and the Union of Soviet Socialist Republics, which are hereby designated the Depositary Governments.

(3) This Convention shall enter into force after the deposit of instruments of ratification by twenty-two Governments, including the Governments designated as Depositaries of the Convention.

(4) For States whose instruments of ratification or accession are deposited subsequent to the entry into force of this Convention, it shall enter into force on the date of the deposit of their instruments of ratification or accession.

(5) The Depository Governments shall promptly inform all signatory and acceding States of the date of each signature, the date of deposit of each instrument of ratification or of accession and the date of the entry into force of this Convention, and of the receipt of other notices.

(6) This Convention shall be registered by the Depositary Governments pursuant to Article 102 of the Charter of the United Nations.

Article XV

This Convention, the English, Russian, French, Spanish and Chinese texts of which are equally authentic, shall be deposited in the archives of the Depositary Governments. Duly certified copies of the Convention shall be transmitted by the Depositary Governments to the Governments of the signatory and acceding states.

IN WITNESS WHEREOF the undersigned, duly authorized, have signed this Convention.

DONE in triplicate, at the cities of Washington, London and Moscow, this tenth day of April, one thousand nine hundred and seventy-two.

Index

A Note on the Author

KATHLEEN C. BAILEY received a Ph.D. from the University of Illinois at Urbana-Champaign and is currently the director of arms control studies at National Security Research in Fairfax, Virginia. She previously was the deputy director of research at the U.S. Information Agency, deputy assistant secretary at the State Department, and assistant director of the Arms Control and Disarmament Agency in Washington, D.C. She lectures widely on the issues of arms control, defense, and public diplomacy.